IMPRINT CLASSICS

Australian Painters in Etaples

JEAN-CLAUDE LESAGE

Translated from French by PAULINE LE BORGNE

ETT IMPRINT
Sydney-Paris Link

Published in Imprint Classics by ETT Imprint in 2025

First published by ETT Imprint, Exile Bay in 2022

First published as *Peintres Australiens a Etaples* by A.M.M.E editions in 2000
English translation by Pauline Le Borgne for A.M.M.E. editions

ETT Imprint, PO Box R1906, Royal Exchange NSW 1225 Australia

ISBN: 978-1-923205-98-7 (Paper)
ISBN: 978-1-922698-44-5 (ebook)

Cover: Isobel Rae, *Rogation Sunday*

(detail),Musee de Touquet.

Cover and design Tom Thompson

A Sydney-Paris Link publication

in memory of Jean-Paul Delamotte

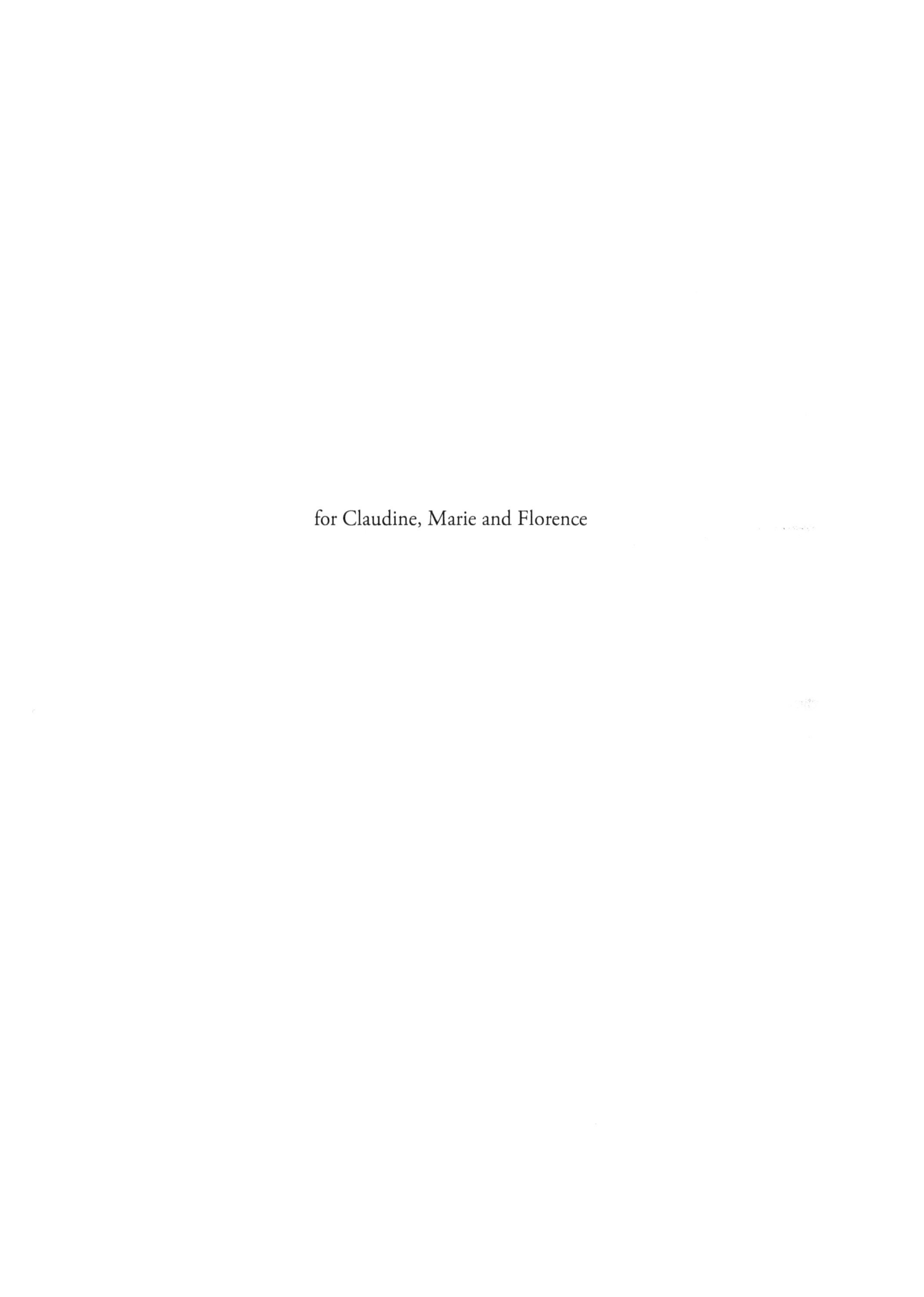

for Claudine, Marie and Florence

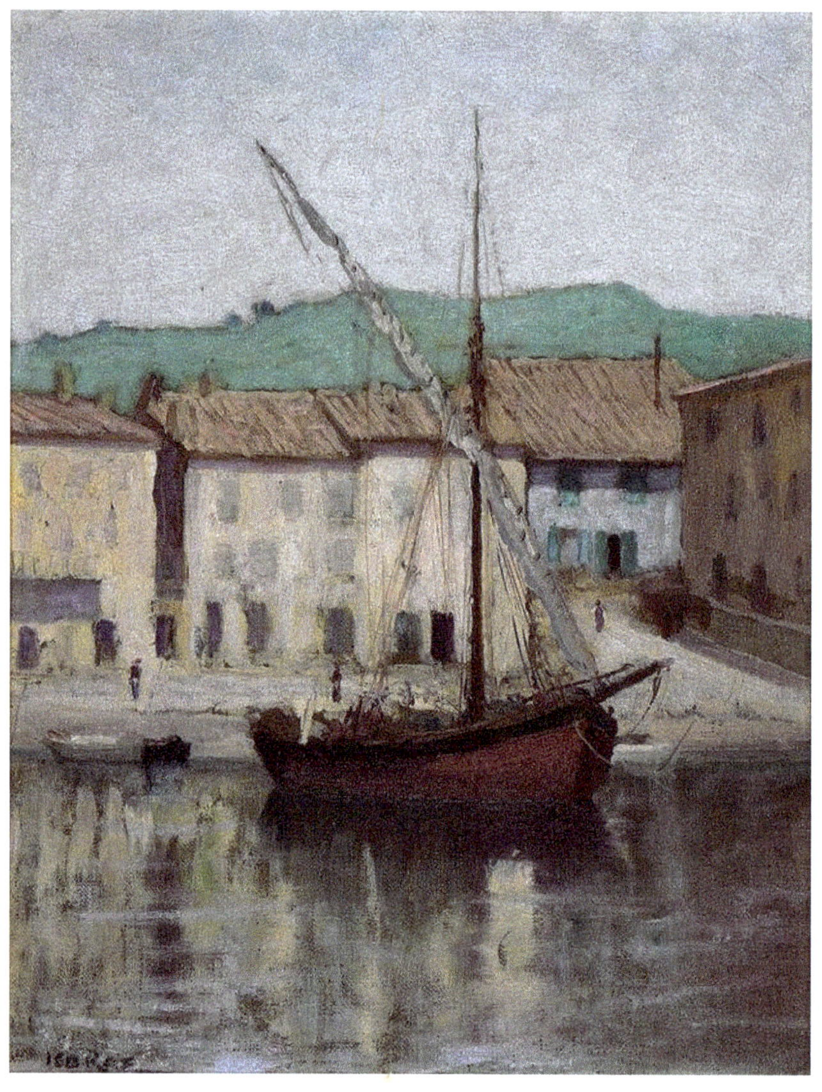

Isobel Rae: *Unitled (Etaples)*, 1912.

CONTENTS

Baker Christina Asquith
Baker Clack Arthur
Bunny Rupert
Bryant Charles
Conder Charles
Dyson Will
Fox Emmanuel Phillips
Fullwood Arthur Henry
Gibson Bessie
Godson John
Hodgkins Frances (NZ)
Honey Winifred
Jenkins Constance (NZ)
Joel Grace (NZ)
Harrison Eleanor Ritchie
Longstaff John
Muskett Alice
Officer Edward Cairns
Quinn James
Rae Alison
Rae Isobel
Rix Nicholas Hilda
Streeton Arthur
Tuck Marie
Tucker Tudor St George

FOREWORD

Australian art is little known in France. One here is ignorant of Tom Roberts, Arthur Streeton or Frederick McCubbin - to name only a few of the impressionists whose works receive public acclaim in Australia.

Before speaking of Australian art, one must determine the cultural background from where it stems and only then can one understand the reasons for the artists coming to Europe, their artistic itineraries and development. They sometimes put down their brushes to take up a pen and recount their adventures in Paris or in "Picardy," at Etaples: like many other artists, the Australian painters could not resist the attraction of a coastal place so close to Paris and its art schools.

The number of Australian artists who came to France around 1900 is surprising with close to thirty alone in Etaples. Some were but tourists and only passed; some, such as Arthur Baker Clack, Rupert Bunny, Isobel Rae, Hilda Rix, Marie Tuck, lingered and their stay in Ecaples marked an important moment in their careers; others became "war artists," painters commissioned by the Australian Government to present testimonies of the cataclysm of the Great War. Alas, with the war, the local artistic activity came to an end: the "Très Riches Heures" of the Etaples School had then been lived.

Except for a few canvases hanging in the Etaples and Le Touquet museums, and an incomplete list of names prepared by Fernand Holuigue[1], a former secretary of the Societe Academique du Touquet, founder and archivist of the Musee du Touquet, almost nothing remains of those glorious years. Therefore, a trip to Australia became necessary and, thanks to the support of the French Embassy in Canberra and the Universite d'Artois, my stay there lasted several months.

Some paintings of Etaples are held in public collections in Australia. In France and in England works also lie in private collections. Five years of research has allowed me to have a fair idea of the chosen topics and the styles practised, as well as the notable influences between the Australian, English and American painters. Didn't they, after all, speak a common language in a foreign country? English enabled certain "elected affinities": Rupert Bunny frequented the Koopmans.[2] Hilda Rix was a friend of Harry Van der Weyden[3] and travelled to Morocco with Henry Ossawa Tanner.[4]

I do not think that any major artist has escaped my investigations. Of course there are other works still to be discovered. Maybe this book will encourage amateurs to bring the works they own to the notice of the public...

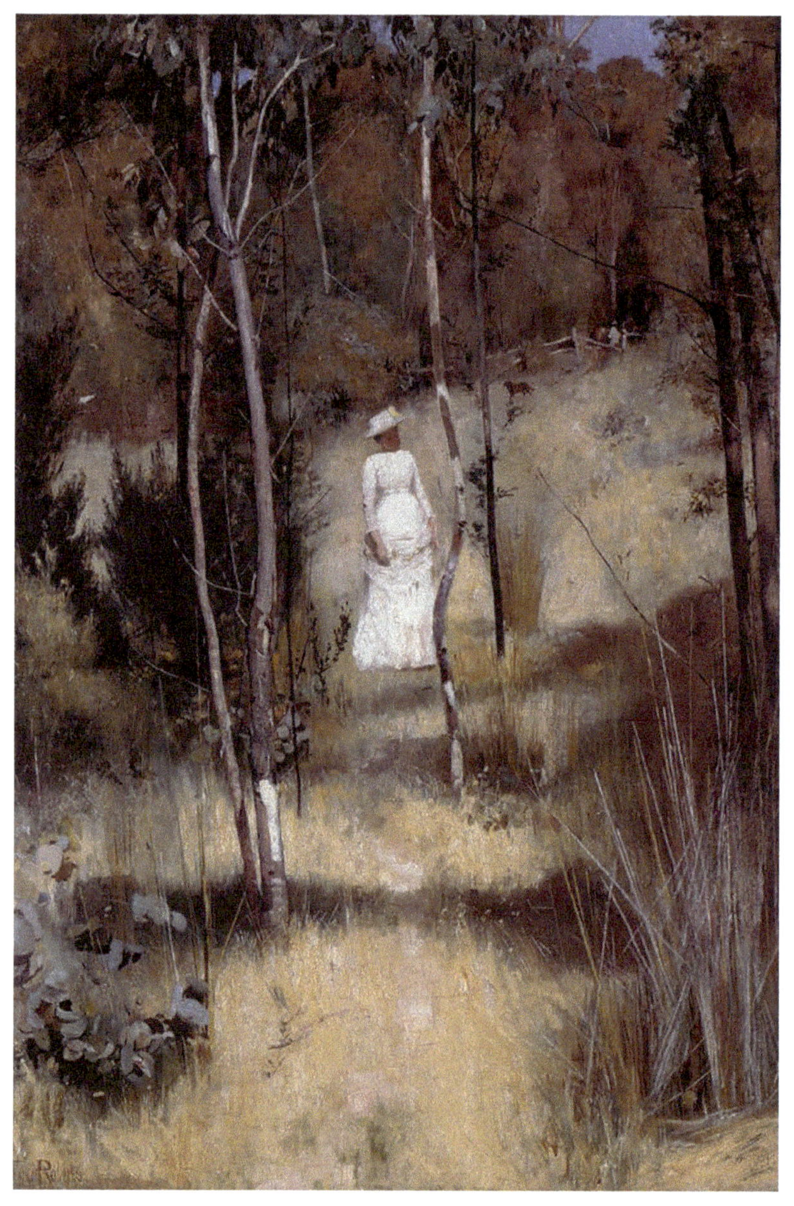

Tom Roberts: *A Summer Morning*, 1886 (Ballarat Fine Art Gallery.

THE IDEA OF PICARDY AT THE TURN OF THE 19TH CENTURY

Until recently, the word "Picardy" represented a territory extending past the Baie de Somme northward to Boulogne, even to Calais. It was customary to use the designation of the "Ancien Règime,"[5] which distinguished Upper Picardy to the south of the Somme, and Lower Picardy to the north. These territories, turned towards the sea, derived their unity not only because of their common history but also, still visible today, because of their landscapes, their activities, their way of living and their language.

These features made little difference to the Anglo-Saxon painters for whom Picardy and Etaples were but one, up to a point that, when reading the word "Picardy" one should have in mind Etaples and its immediate neighbourhood. As early as 1820, R. Parkes Bonington located his picture *Coast of Picardy* near Boulogne. Birge Harrison spoke of Etaples, "on the Picardy coast, as the last and in many respects, the best area in France for artists." *The Craftsman* added that "Etaples, in Picardy, [was] a country of dreams where artists could find countless painting subjects." And *The Painters of Picardy* was the joyful hymn of the Australian painters in Etaples...

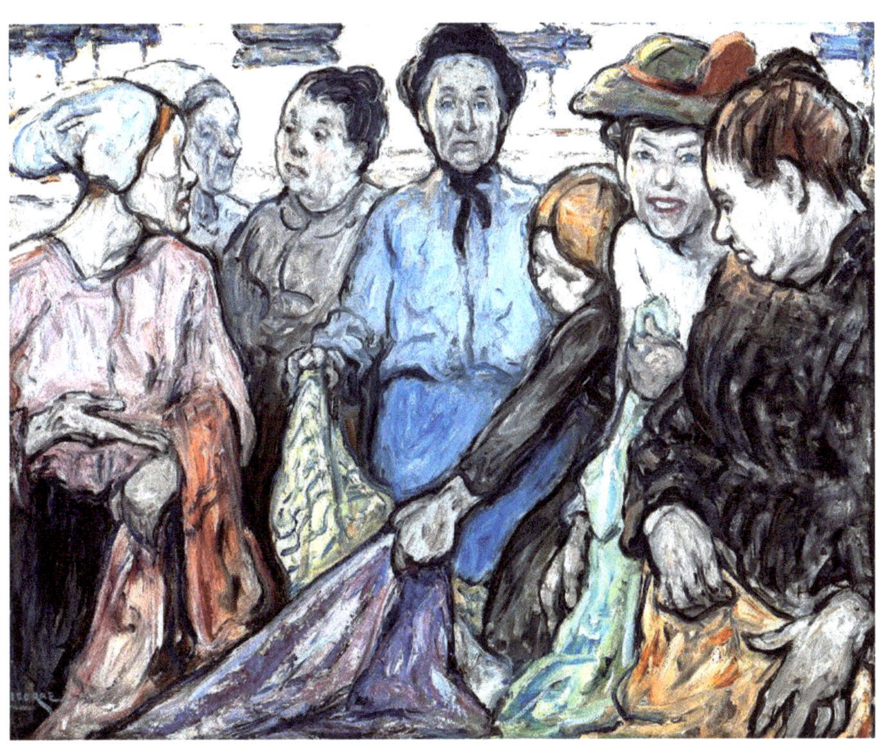

Isobel Rae: *The Marketplace, Etaples,* 1913.

THE PICARDIANS

Pioneer Painting

In the second half of the 19th c., landscape was the "genre" the best represented in Australian painting. The pioneers expected Eugene Von Guerard and Nicolas Chevalier[6] to produce large mountainous landscapes and plains lit by the rays of the setting sun - grandiose and romantic visions close to those of Frederic Edwin Church and Albert Bierstadt.[7] This official form of art was expressed in institutions, major museums and affiliated art schools. George Frederick Folingsby, director of the National Gallery School of Melbourne,[8] encouraged his students to look for new subjects on which to work.

The situation evolved decisively around 1880 when young artists like Tom Roberts, Arthur Streeton, Charles Conder and Frederick McCubbin began the habit of meeting in " bush camps." They discussed theory and studied the effects of light in order to transpose the specific colours of the Australian continent onto the canvas and painted "en plein air." Box Hill and Eaglemont, near Heidelberg (Victoria), were the Pontoise and Argenteuil of the Antipodes. The "Heidelberg School" still conveys today Australian impressionist painting. Tom Roberts was the instigator of the movement. He followed in the footsteps of Louis Buvelot[9] who, before him, had introduced into his lively landscapes some- thing of the familiarity and simplicity of a Corot. At the same time - in 1886, the last impressionist exhibition was held in Paris and new tendencies began to emerge in France: Georges Seurat exhibited *Un Dimanche à la Grande jatte* (Sunday at the Grande Jatte), and Paul Signac, Les Gazometres, Clichy (Gasometers, Clichy).

In 1888, Charles Conder exhibited *Departure of the S. S. Orient, Circular Quay*, a view from above which pushes the horizon to the top of the canvas, expanding the space. The subtle grey tones, sharpened by touches of red, the wet quays, the pattern of the umbrellas, all show unmistakably impressionism, in the manner of Girolamo Nerli.[10] The purchase of the work by the Sydney Museum was a sign of recognition of the new Australian painting. The young painters gained confidence and in 1889, Roberts, Conder, Streeton and McCubbin organised an exhibition in Melbourne entitled the "'9x5' Impression Exhibition." The figures relate to the dimensions in "inches" of the lids of the cigar boxes on which Roberts and friends dashed off their "impressions of the moment." For a good number of historians, the exhibition marked the birth of Australian "plein air" painting. Yet, to stray from the academic style was risky; therefore and in order to survive, a number of young painters were first and foremost portrait artists or cartoonists, even photographers.

Little by little, however, recognised institutions became aware of a genuine Australian art movement. Nationalism was in the air. In 1901 it culminated in the federation of six colonies into one fully-fledged nation. It created a blossoming birth and an explosion of talent: the National Gallery of Victoria was already offering gifted students travelling scholarships to complete their training in art schools in Europe. A selected student received a grant of £150 over three years. In return, three works, of which two were to be copies after masters, and one of a personal inspiration, had to be achieved.[11] From now on, young artists for whom art was a total commitment and not a "pastime for young ladies" - as Conder put it, would have their eyes fixed on Europe, London, and above all, Paris - the centre of true artistic life, "the Mecca of the arts..."

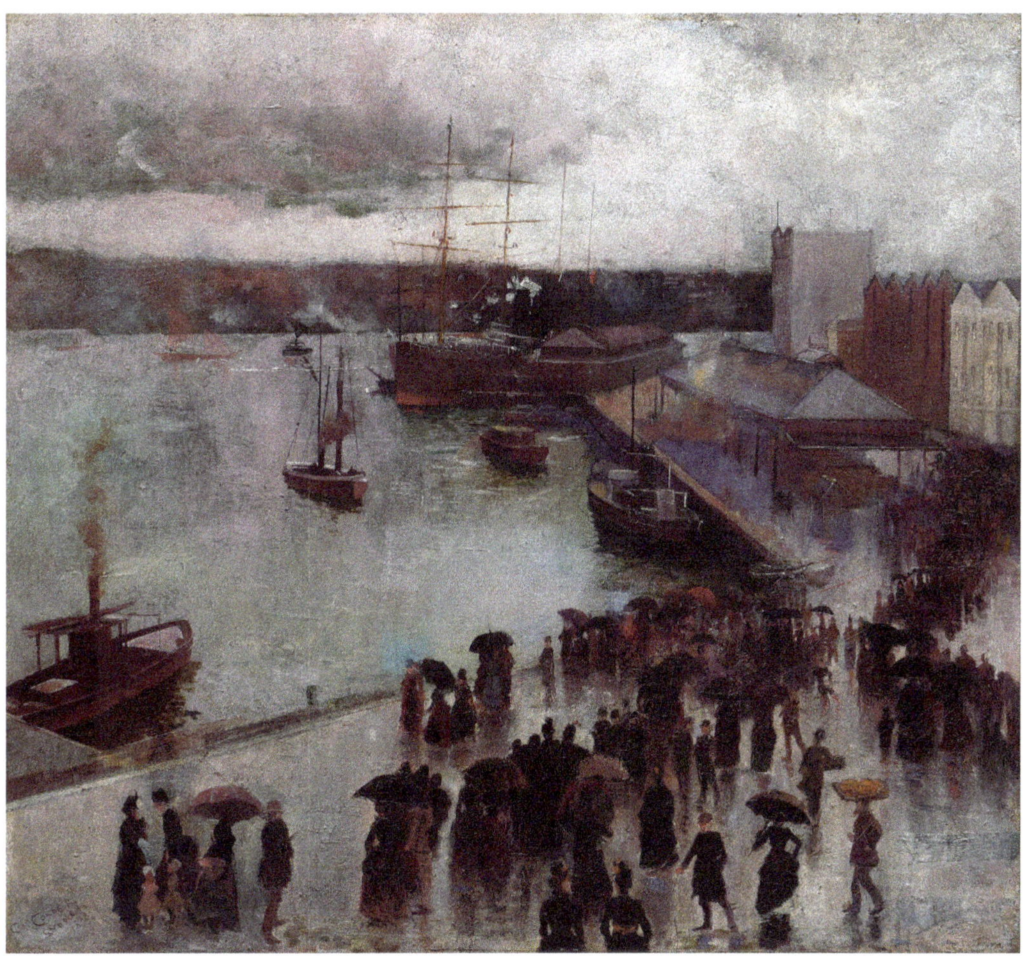

Charles Conder: *Departure of the S.S. Orient, Circular Quay,* 1888. Art Gallery of NSW.

Off to Europe, for the Love of Art

The departure of artists for Europe became a regular habit. Their professors had trained in London, Paris or Munich, and all these young people dreamt, in turn, of the *Royal Academy* and of the Paris Salon.

The first wave of Australian painters, Tom Roberts, John Peter Russell, Charles Richardson, Rupert Bunny, arrived in London between 1881 and 1885. They enrolled in the schools of the *Royal Academy* and the *Slade*, where Alphonse Legros professed "memory-training theories": to observe and memorise scenes and subjects which could be used when painting. They then felt ready to go to Paris and confront the Salon Jury.

Those who followed later, John Longstaff, Charles Conder, E. Phillips Fox, Tudor St. George Tucker, James Quinn, Isobel Rae, went directly to Paris. They enrolled at the Académie Julian or "chez Colarossi" where they were prepared for the Salon and the Ecole des Beaux-Arts. Not only were Australians attracted by France: pilgrim artists flowed from the four corners of the world and Americans by the hundreds. The French looked disapprovingly at the studios invaded by athletic, bohemian artists who spoke loudly and drank tea all day.

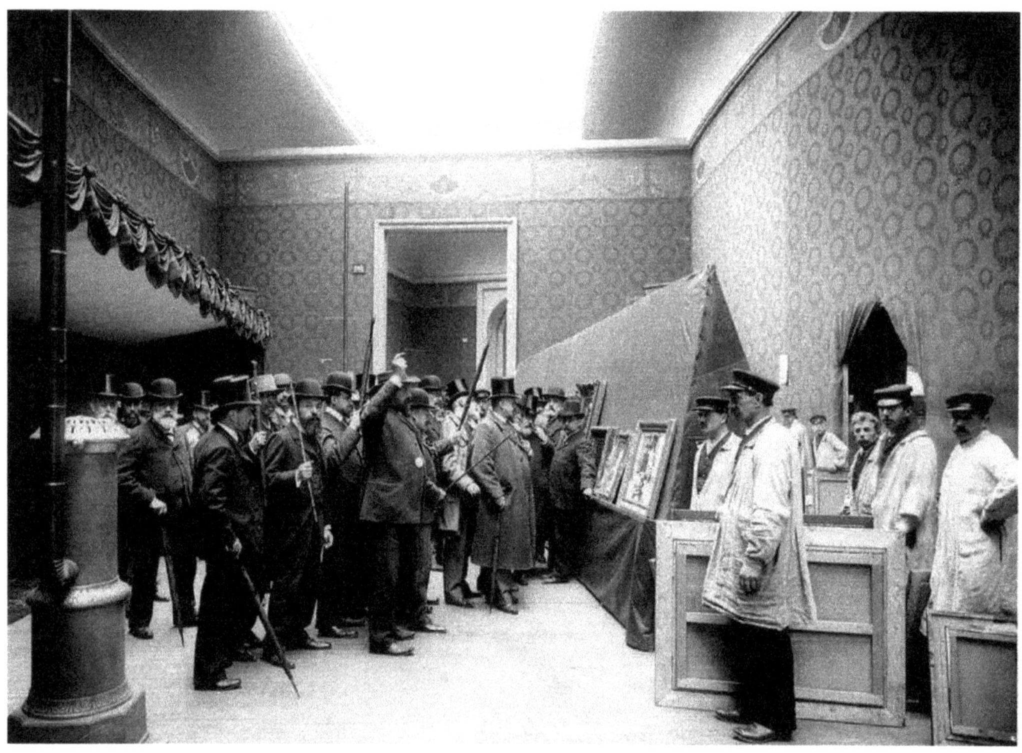

Jury at the Paris Salon, 1903.

These students, who came to Paris in the hope of making a career had, firstly, to familiarise themselves with the institutions and the art world. They willingly submitted to the rules so as to attract the attention of the Salon jury. After all, were they not among the 4,000 candidates expecting recognition and to see their work hanging on "the line?" "The army of foreign artists in Paris is legion. And amongst them, gathered together for study, no more earnest workers are to be found than our own little group of Australian artists. None can be said to be more united, freer from petty jealousies, more generously helpful towards one another when things are inclined to go wrong: without an exception, more delighted over each other's successes, either in private work or public exhibition. And whilst it still comes as a surprise to many that so young a country as ours should show artistic tendencies... We must confess that, considering the art future of Victoria from the starting point of those works that we have been exhibited on the walls of the Salons and the Royal Academy, the outlook is, to an astonishing degree, brilliant... For whether the studio attended be Cormon's at Montmartre, where Mr Longstaff works, Colarossi's of the Grande Chaumiere (see below), to which Mr Bunny belongs, or Colarossi of the avenue Victor Hugo where Miss Rae studies, the hours are the same - 8 to 12 in the morning and 1 to 5 in the afternoon. Rather different from the 10 o'clock start in our own school."[12]

The professors, painters of renown, would go once or twice a week to the studios to correct work. "After lengthy studies, one's painting is submitted to the jury of the Paris Salon. Then follow the days of waiting, when hope and fear play hot havoc with the brain. The rumour flutters around the circle of one's friends that 'A' has heard results - that he is 'thrown' and that 'B' has been accepted. When the postman (whose coming you have wooed, yet feared) hands you the envelope containing the printed announcement which informs you of your fate, even before you open it, you can see the colour of the paper within. If green, it thrusts you into a despair so far-reaching that it seems fatal. But... but... if it is pink! - the gods are good, your heart leaps for joy, your pulses beat a loud tattoo, and you would even (but for a saving discretion) hug the old postman."[13] Only then is one able to climb the steps of the Palais des Champs-Elysees, heart beating, in search of one's work, hanging alongside some of the most famous works of the century.

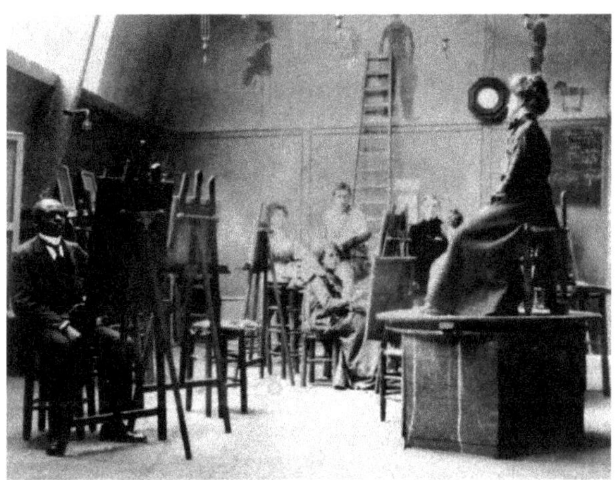

Women also...

Among the thirty or so Australian artists who were in Picardy, half were women. They were made up of a very specific element: those who left their country for Europe were young, energetic women endowed with strong characters and an independent nature. They possessed that pioneer spirit which allowed them to take risks over and above the rules. The bad reputation of the Paris art scene at the time encouraged parents to chaperone their offspring. Isobel Rae was one of the first Australian artists to come to France with her mother and sister. Of the long list of artist travellers: Ethel Carrick Fox, Stella Bowen, Maud Burge, Alice Chapman, Bessie Davidson, Frances Hodgkins, Bessie Gibson, Dora Meeson, Hilda Rix, Marie Tuck, one striking figure emerges - that of Margaret Preston. She made the most of two long stays in Paris, visiting the major collections, taking courses at the Musée Guimet where she studied Japanese art, becoming familiar with all forms of major work. In Adelaide, she did much for the recognition of an independent Australian art and, finding her inspiration in the cultural depths of her country, she was one of the first to identify the importance of Aboriginal art; also the first to open a school where anatomical study was done with the nude figure.

The trends

Impressionism, of all the movements, was the one that had the most impact amongst the Australian artists. Cubism does not seem to have retained their attention. As for Expressionism, it exists naturally in the violent and often hostile red continent and traces are to be found in all Australian 20th c. art - strongly expressed in the works of Sydney Nolan, Arthur Boyd and John Perceval. The recent rediscovery of Aboriginal art shows the same sensitivity.

Australian painting achieved its identity when its most talented artists left their native country in search of training and culture, and thus won the freedom to create. For many of them, to reach Europe was a voyage of initiation into the world of art. Far from doing copies, the contact with European "pictorial revolutions" was the revelation of their own abilities, their real nature, as well as an incredible stimulant. And in this cauldron of ideas and theories, the real creators found their way and the means of surpassing themselves.

"Etaples, that happy hunting ground for so many artists" [14]

Throughout the 19th c., the coasts of the English Channel attracted many land and sea-scape painters.[15] They were the travelling painters who, like R. Parkes Bonington, explored the coast from Calais to Normandy, without restriction. In Etaples, things were different and the focus was on the birth of an artistic centre where painters spent one or a few summers, one or a number of years, or even finished their days there.

"We owe our introduction to Etaples, to the house we inhabit, to its proprietor - as well as to models and townspeople - to two artist friends now in Melbourne, who worked here for eighteen months and who endeavoured to persuade us that the country was preferable to Paris during the winter. Our first descent at the railway station was on a gloomy evening at the close of June. We left Paris in sunshine to discover that it had been raining all day in the north. Etaples was veiled in mist, her tiled roofs dripping, and the streets in a condition to render walking decidedly unpleasant... We came out upon the long triangular Etaples Place, close beside a group of wind-distorted plane trees... In another moment, we arrived at our destination, and in less than half-an-hour were comfortably established in the rooms lately occupied by our friends... We found evidence of their presence, not only in the art decorations and materials with which the cupboards were filled, but in the Australian books and familiar gum leaves the secretaire [16] contained."[17]

Alison and Isobel Rae were directed to Mme Pannier who possessed one of the most sought after studios in town. Its situation on the market place a few steps from the fishing harbour, represented a good address which was passed on to other painters. At the back were gardens onto rue du Bae, with a large studio constructed by Birge Harrison.[18] The two sisters took their meals and lodged with Mme Cresson.

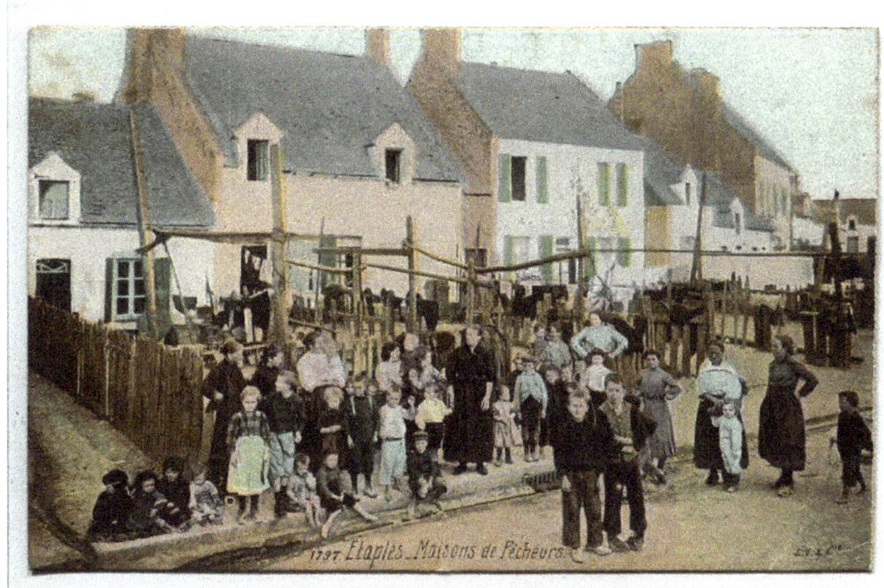

Twelve years later, the charm had not disappeared and Elsie Rix would remember: "On the farthest side of the station are grey stone windmills; chalk quarries and hills geometrically laid out in crops, curving white roads and distant pine trees. In the opposite direction is the sweet silvery hamlet of Trépied, almost entirely peopled by artists who have made most delectable little homes out of the peasants' cottages. Further on still are the sand dunes of Cucq - great hills of pale creamy sand set in soft green meadow country... Beyond are more and more sand dunes, stretching far into the distance to the low-lying silver of the sea."[19]

The River Canche, and its luminous estuary, was the main reason for attracting painters to Etaples. Victor Hugo introduced the theme in 1837 as "one of the most gracious little gulfs of the Channel." Emmanuel Damoye, Karl Daubigny, and especially Eugène Boudin,[20] gave the site its notoriety. Since then numerous paintings have depicted the Canche from all angles, in all weathers and seasons: from the bridge on the river near the mouth or from the south bank, through the pines - either by Rupert Bunny or by Arthur Baker Clack.

The view from the north bank of the Canche and the port of Etaples was another subject favoured by the painters. Around 1910, the fishing fleet numbered about sixty boats, mostly luggers. Nearby land today used for parking, was an area of permanent activity: shipbuilding, slips, repair workshops and mending of nets. Life was lived with the rhythm of the tides and when the fish market bell announced the return of the fishermen, women and children came running whether it be to greet a husband, a father, a brother or a son, or to help in the unloading of the fish in the large, rustic, traditional baskets: a multitude of subjects for painting and sketching, such as can be seen in Marie Tuck's works which, almost 100 years later and aside from their pictorial qualities, present an undeniable ethnographic character.

The Grand-Place also drew the painters. They would sketch the Town Hall, the small provincial "Balzacian" building, while a verse of The Picardy Painters sung out the nervous activity of the market days: "On a market day / The Place is full of sketching / Some in oil they say / Some are doing etching / Some in aquarelle / Some in pastels mellow / Some in crayon noir / Some in crayon mellow. CHORUS. We're the Brothers of the Brush / We're Picardian painters / To Etaples we all rush / To paint peasants just as quaint as / Can be - can be / The peasants of Picardy / Yips, yips, yips, tra, la, la, tra, la." [21]

Etaples was also known for its numerous cheap artists' models - a paradise for painters. "Etaples, upon the coast of Picardy is the latest and in many respects, the best of the artist resorts of France. Situated twenty miles south of Boulogne, upon the main line from Paris to London, it lies just at the point where the rails swerve away from the rather desolate shore and sweep inland to Amiens. Etaples does not attract at first sight. It does better. It attracts gradually and by degrees, and grows upon one at last so that it has already become an axiom among the artists that he who stays a week will stay for years."[22]

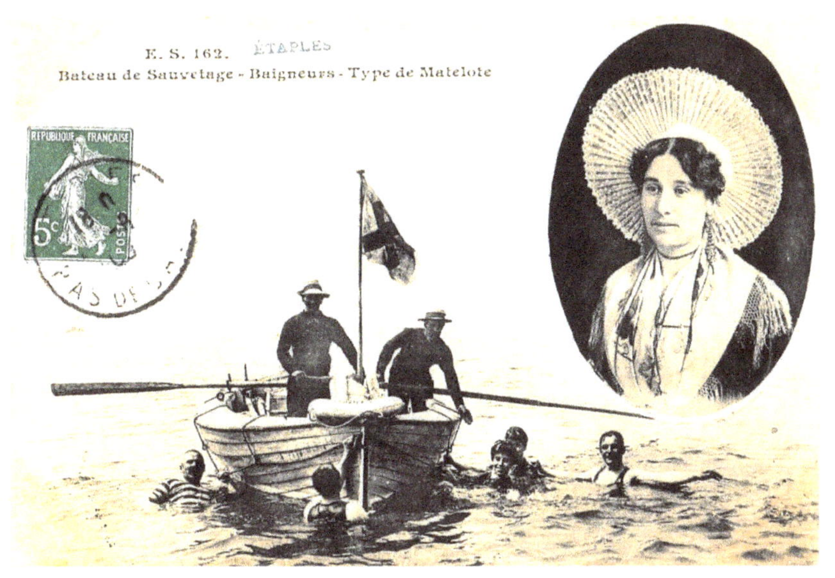
E. S. 162. ÉTAPLES
Bateau de Sauvetage - Baigneurs - Type de Matelote
RÉPUBLIQUE FRANÇAISE
5c
POSTES

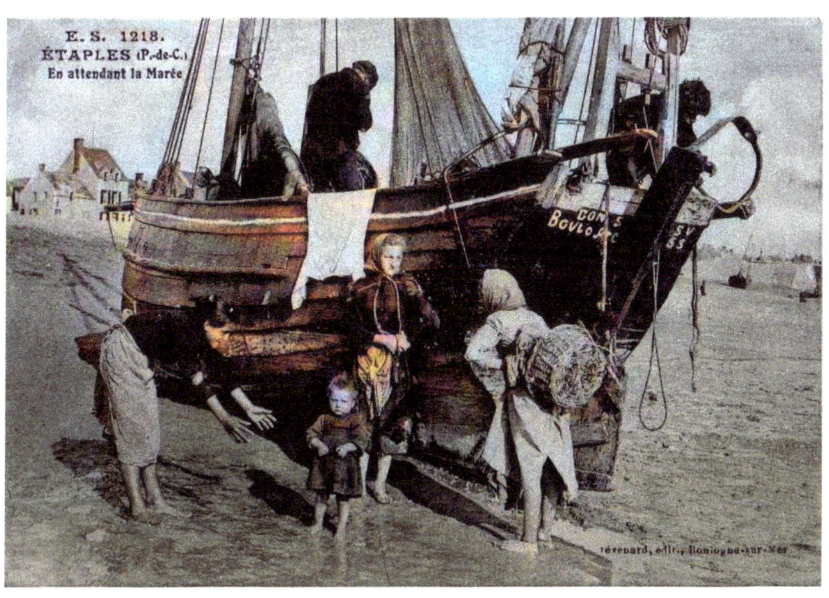
E. S. 1218.
ÉTAPLES (P.-de-C.)
En attendant la Marée
évenard, édit., Boulogne-sur-Mer

In the end, the inhabitants became used to the presence of the artists. They frequented them daily and eventually were not surprised by the foreign accents heard in the shops, at the market or in the port. They benefited from the presence of the artistic colony in renting rooms and studios, and selling artists' material. Dr Dacquet, an emblematic personality and local donor, encouraged and facilitated artistic creativity. He had built, at the back of his garden, a small house facing the rue des Violiers, with two rooms on the ground floor, and a large well-lit room on the first floor. Iso Rae occupied this lodging for a number of years.

The Hotel Ioos, on the Grand-Place, was the general meeting place for transient painters. Those who lodged in other boarding houses - rue du Rivage, rue d'Hérambault or rue de Montreuil, would meet there for long convivial evenings. No artist would omit the ritualistic evenings at the hotel, run by the Alsacian Antoine Ioos and his wife, Anna. The artists felt at home amid paintings hanging side by side, according to the shape of the wall and the space available. More than one artist paid his bill in kind, in what was to become the first museum of the Etaples School. When the French State bought *Le Grand Marche à Tanger* by Hilda Rix, in 1912, the "Artist Colony of Etaples" met at Hotel Ioos on 5 December. Anselme, the "garcon" of the hotel, with the help of the maid, Helene, set thirty three places. The event was celebrated with dignity. All the painters and their spouses signed the congratulatory card addressed to Hilda Rix and intoned the hymn: "We're the Brothers of the Brush..."[23]

Some documents and photographs also recall the souvenir of promenades at the seaside, of picnics, and fancy dress balls. Some outings were organised to Montreuil: they took the train from Etaples and half an hour later they were in Montreuil. Close to the "Porte de Boulogne" was the private residence of Harry Van der Weyden. The happy band would make merry in the shady garden, while at the same time admiring the elegant sports car owned by their rich friend, before entering the studio to comment on his latest work.

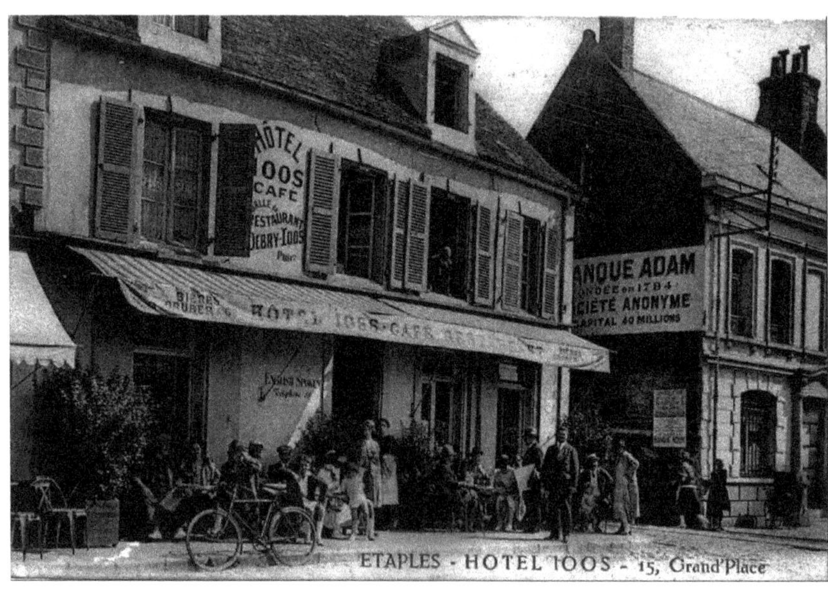

ETAPLES - HOTEL IOOS - 15, Grand'Place

With the flow of artists, la Societe des Amis des Arts organised painting exhibitions - the first being held at the Etaples Town Hall in 1892. Forty-five artists participated: Iso Rae, Eugène Boudin, Henri Duhem, Louis Paul Dessar.[24] To give the event an official and solemn character, Eugene Chigot and Louis Le Sidaner[25] requested the patronage of the Minister of Education and Fine Arts, the President of the Conseil General and the Sous-Préfet. Eugene Chigot, promoter of the arts in Etaples and member of the City Council, obtained for the opening - set for 7 August - a vast programme of activities with concerts, bicycle races and yachting regattas on the River Canche. An intimate dinner in the evening assembled Messrs the Sous-Préfet, Chigot, Le Sidaner, Duhem and Thaulow[26] at the Lion d'Or restaurant... And the Sous-Préfet's speech ascertained that, "In the district of Montreuil and at Etaples at the "Lion d'Or," at Ioos's, or at Maure's,[27] one would think one was in London, Glasgow, or New York. It is why I drink a toast to the foreign artists living in the district of Montreuil and, particularly, to the Norwegian master who has been on holiday for a few weeks in the village of Camiers, Mr Thaulow..." And Chigot, continuing after the Sous-Prefer, emphasised the conviviality of the artistic colony: "What draws and retains the painters in Etaples is not only the beauty of the surrounding sights, the admirable sunsets over the sea, the bay so interesting when moonlit, and the shadows of the pine forest which produce such striking effects, it is above all, yourselves, my dear friends."[28]

Later, from 1896, the exhibitions were held at Paris-Plage.[29] In the new seaside resort, the artists found a location adapted to their needs and eventual buyers. Thus, they continued to paint in Etaples, in Trépied, in Montreuil, but exhibited and sold in Paris-Plage. The new Societe Artistique de Picardie held its first exhibition in 1904, at the Chateau du Touquet-Paris-Plage. That of 1909 was a success, reported a local newspaper: "We have the pleasure to inform our readers that the French, English and American exhibition, organised by the Etaples and Montreuil schools, will open in the parish hall, rue de Londres, Tuesday 27 July. The official opening will be held the evening before. Some eminent artists have sent canvases from the Royal Academy and other distinguished English academies."[30]

Iso Rae, Edward Officer, James Quinn, Rupert Bunny, Marie Tuck actively participated in the local exhibitions. Arthur Baker Clack was a member of the jury, while Hilda Rix prepared a large poster in colour for the Salon des Beaux-Arts.

The Anglo-Saxons at large chaired committees and cook part in the organisation and development of such exhibitions.[31] In 1913 and 1914 the catalogue became more professional and contained photographic reproductions.[32] But the Great War brought a fatal blow to the artistic life. Abandoning their studios, the painters regained their countries in a rush. It was the end of working for exhibitions. Henceforth, recruitment was for "War Artists."

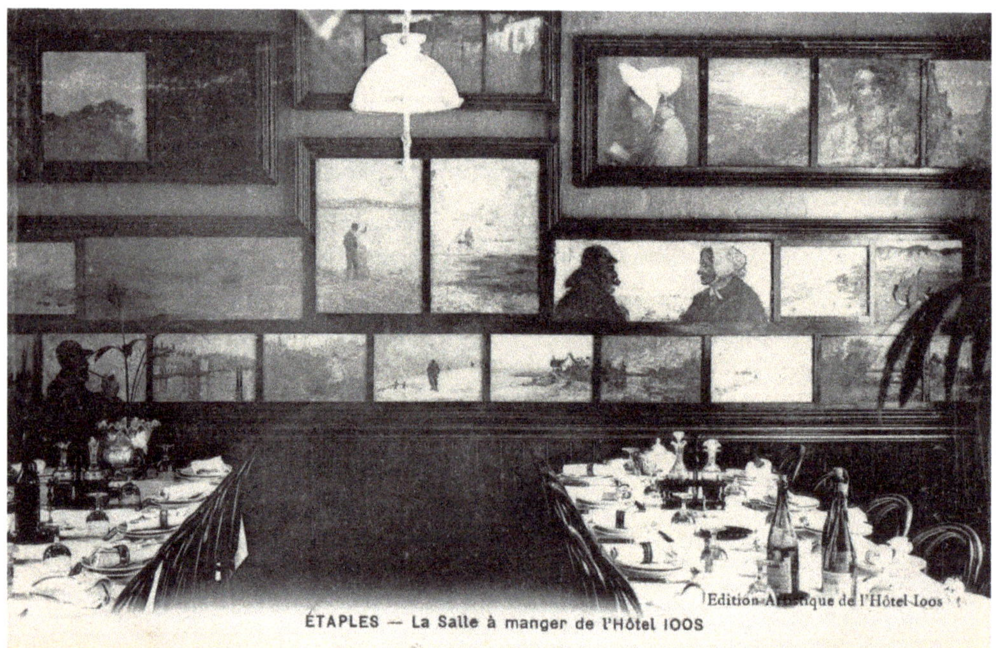

Several of Iso Rae's studies of local fisher folk can be seen in the Hotel Ioo's postcard from 1910.

Hilda Rix Nicholas painted this poster for the 1913 Salon des Beaux Arts event during her stay at Etaples.

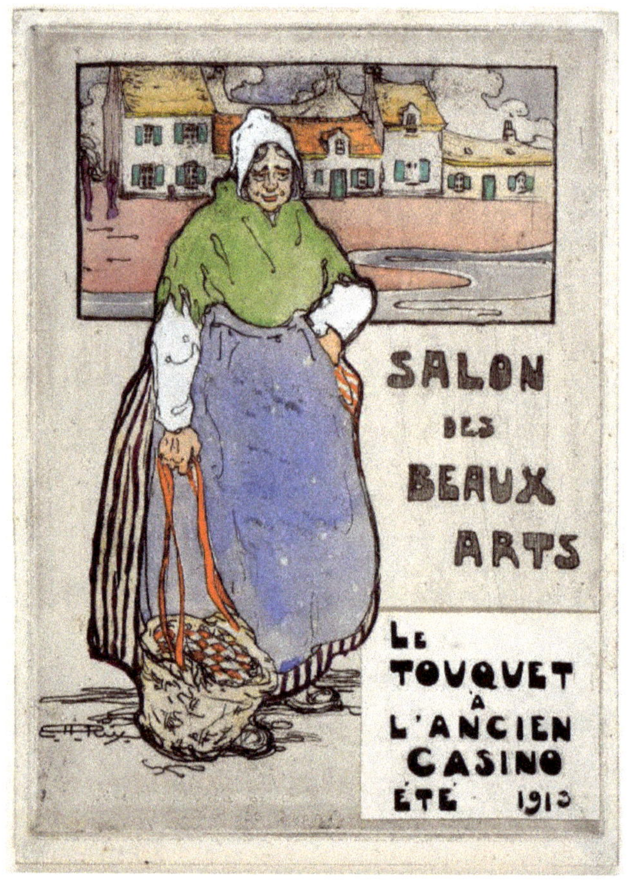

ARTHUR BAKER CLACK

"One has to steer one's course as well as one can in the seas of conflicting ideas. The experience of 20 years' practice has led me to believe in Bernard Shaw that the only rule about art is that there is none. Rupert Bunny, most sympathetic of teachers, gave me sound advice at the beginning. Then I did the academic stunt for some time at Julian's under the great Jean-Paul Laurens, whose honest principles about drawing were a good foundation from which to experiment in other directions, very dissimilar but undoubtedly, equally honest. From Steinlen, supremely clever as an illustrator of the life of the people in Paris, I received encouragement to work out my own artist salvation with the result that every picture I paint is a new and fascinating problem."

Arthur Baker Clack[33]

Arthur Baker Clack studied at Way College, Adelaide. After holding various jobs in Western Australia, he became a reporter on the Perth *Morning Herald* His adventurous spirit was stirred by the discovery of gold in Coolgardie, which had made the whole country feverish. But little by little his desire to become a painter emerged, a desire so strong that in 1906 Baker Clack left for Europe - an eventful voyage as the vessel was shipwrecked off the Cornish coast.

In Paris he entered the Académie Julian and associated with fellow countryman, Rupert Bunny, whose reputation was already established and who had a studio at 24 boulevard des Invalides. It is to Bunny that Baker Clack owed his colourful palette. Jean-Paul Laurens[34] taught him the art of drawing, but Baker Clack had a strong enough personality to free himself of the influence of he who had painted the *Excommunication de Robert le Pieux ...*

It is often the period of early enthusiasm and fortuitous meetings which decides the orientation of a career. Théophile Alexandre Steinlen,[35] painter of Paris life, encouraged the artist's early beginnings. Baker Clack discovered the work of Seurat and Cezanne who became new references and examples to follow. With Cezanne recently deceased, the 1907 Salon d'Automne presented a noteworthy retrospective focusing attention on the Aix-en-Provence master. Soon after his marriage to Edith Smith, a young English woman, Baker Clack settled in Etaples and exhibited regularly at Le Touquet. The local press was kind but surprised by his bold technique: "With spirit, youthfulness and originality, Baker Clack will make his way if he hasn't already done so."[36]

Baker Clack practised still-life and landscapes with equal success: the port of Etaples, the boats at the quay-side, the ship-building yards (of which there are a number of versions) - all served to inspire him. There also exist views of the town and the surrounding countryside: Trépied, Cucq, Saint-Josse, the Camiers dunes, Merlimont and Marenla. With his flamboyant palette, Baker Clack dared to paint Etaples with the range of colours used by the Fauves at

Collioure in the South of France. His canvases also recall those by Vlaminck painted at Chatou near Paris. The boldness of tones gives at times an unreal character to the painting, notably in *Bateaux en chantier.* In *Panier de fleurs*, the strokes juxtapose squares of colourful matter and Van Gogh is not far when, with thick layers of paint, Baker Clack searches for vibration by modulating the greens, the blues and the yellows to attain a true, personal expression. Far from the impressionist vision of many of the Etaples painters, French or foreign, Baker Clack shows a sensibility which I would willingly qualify as "Australian," bringing his palette to an even stronger range such as one can see in *Les Dunes de Camiers.*

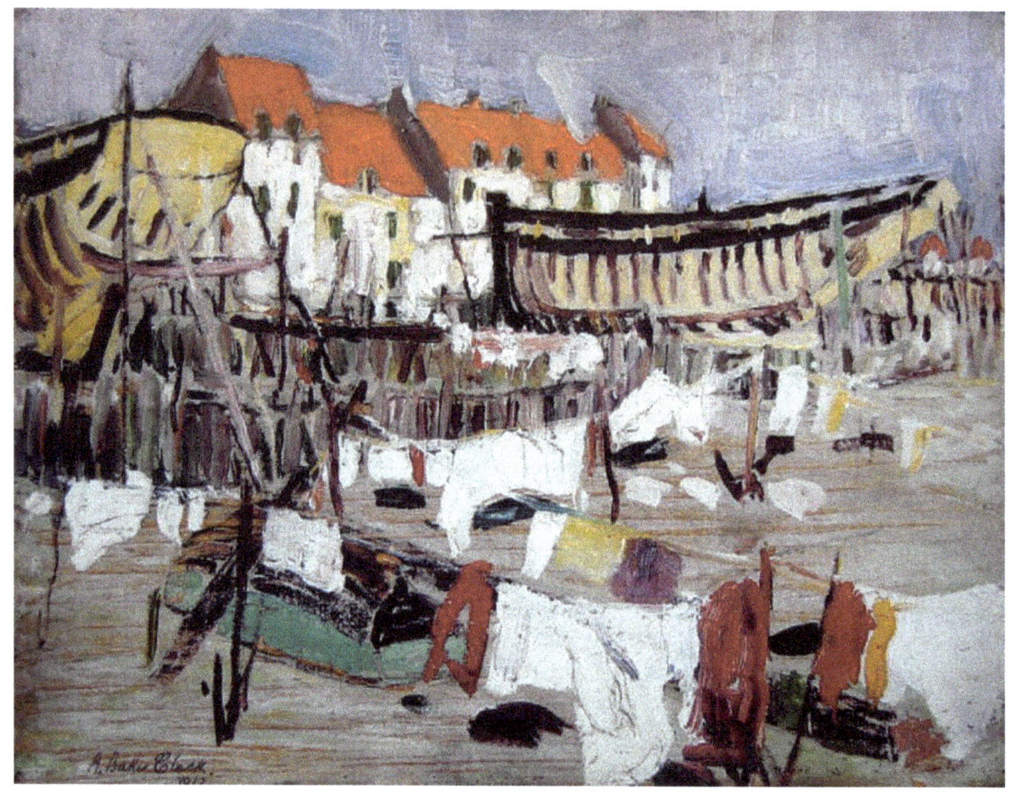

Arthur Baker Clack: *Bateaux en chantier* (preparatory work, 1914).

The construction of boats in the port of Etaples offered a scene of activity to the passer-by and retained the attention of the painter. Here Baker Clack fully seizes all the aesthetic aspects in this preparatory work which shows the major elements - composition and a colourful range. Even if he is to add a few details in the final work, the essential rests. He worked generously in undiluted paint. Only an Australian would be able to render the Etaples sky with its mosaic of blues tinged with pink and violet. With its striking foreground of a seashore, overturned green dinghy, washing in an undefined form, there is almost an element of movement. From the preparatory work to the finished painting it is very difficult to make a choice, so appealing are the two works in their own ways.

During the First World War, Baker Clack served in the Allied International Forces, his wife doing voluntary work in the canteens of the Australian regiments in the Etaples Camp along with Iso Rae.[37] But, as early as 1919, Baker Clack returned to his brushes and the exhibition trail. As his accommodation in Etaples had been destroyed by bombardments, he chose to relocate in Trépied. In Chemin Dusannier, he occupied some disused military barracks which, when enlarged and reorganised became a charming cottage. *The Home*, an Australian magazine, recounts "the cosily arranged living-room and its antique furnishings ..." and a photograph shows Baker Clack at the Hotel de France in Montreuil-sur-Mer in the company of his wife and Mrs George Patterson, wife of his friend and first biographer.[38] Apart from local exhibitions, Baker Clack participated in the Salon d'Automne, the Salon des Independants and the Salon de la Societe Nationale des Beaux-Arts. In London, like many fellow Australians, he exhibited at the Beaux-Arts Gallery and the Faculty of Arts Gallery. The years 1920 to 1930 correspond with the artist's maturity and exhibition catalogues give proof of abundant production: numerous paintings were shown in Paris, London, Le Touquet and Sydney. His work has, however, remained virtually unknown. His strong personality and the originality of his production contributed to it staying off the beaten track. Baker Clack always held art in the highest esteem throughout his life. Often his scruples or qualms of conscience with regard to parting with his canvases would lead him to go as far as saying to a prospective buyer that the painting was not for sale!

Baker Clack was one of the pillars of the Etaples artistic colony. He and his wife enjoyed the social life and would participate in numerous gatherings of the "Brothers of the Brush." As an Australian used to vast spaces, he loved the out-door life and, installed in the precarious, wicker sidecar, would cover the countryside in the company of Jules Wengel (below)[39] or go to Le Touquet to swim with friends. The man whose friends called "Clicky," frequented the Etaples area for almost a quarter of a century and finally left for England in 1934, finishing his life in Kent.

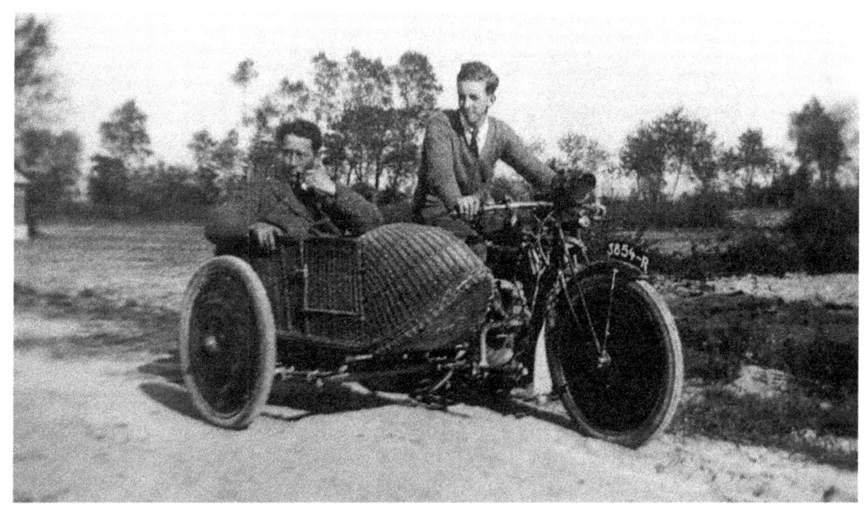

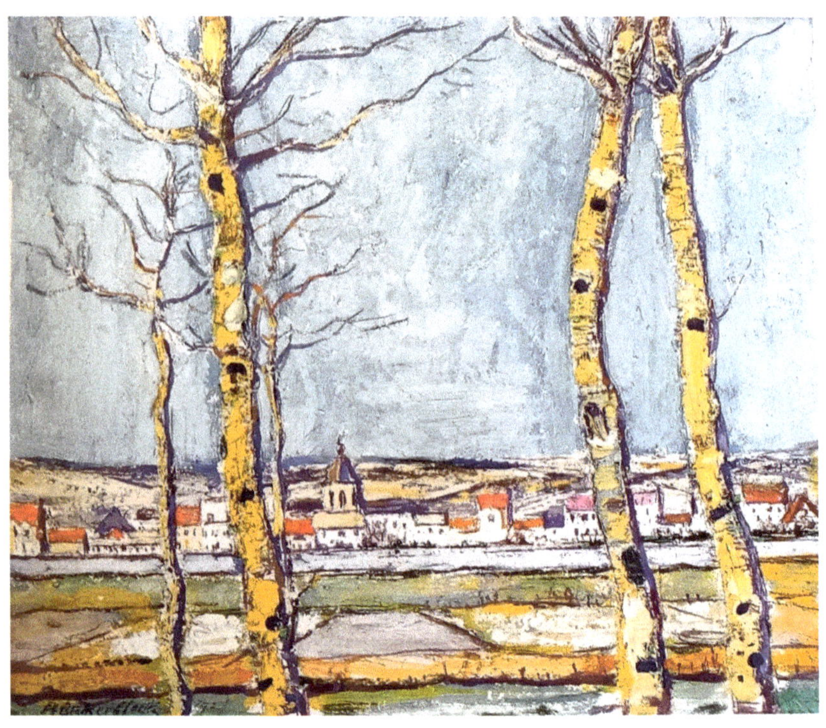

Arthur Baker Clack: *Paysages*

These three landscapes deal with the common theme of houses seen through trees not unlike the view by Pissarro in his *Toits rouges* and his Pontoise landscapes, or that of Cezanne's painting *La Maison du pendu*, (*The House of the Hanged*), in Auvers-sur-Oise - both references which Baker Clack often quoted. However, throughout the theme, his process evolves: the almost monochrome impasto applied with palette knife of *Inondations à Trépied,* gives way to in *Vue de village ou les Toits rouges*, an emphasis of modulated light.

With *Paysage d'Etaples* (ca. 1921), Baker Clack's palette sobers. The painter's eye has familiarised with the luminous subtleties of the French coast and forgotten the contrasting force of the Australian nature. The work suggests a view in delicate nuances and with great clarity, overall tempered where only the patches of the red-tiled roofs are reminiscent of his earlier, bold beginnings.

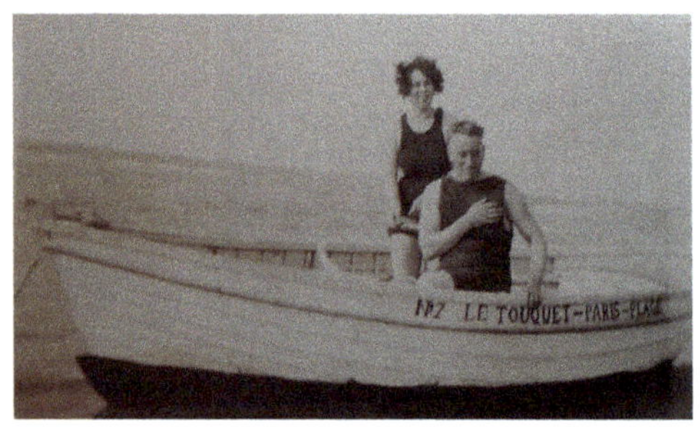

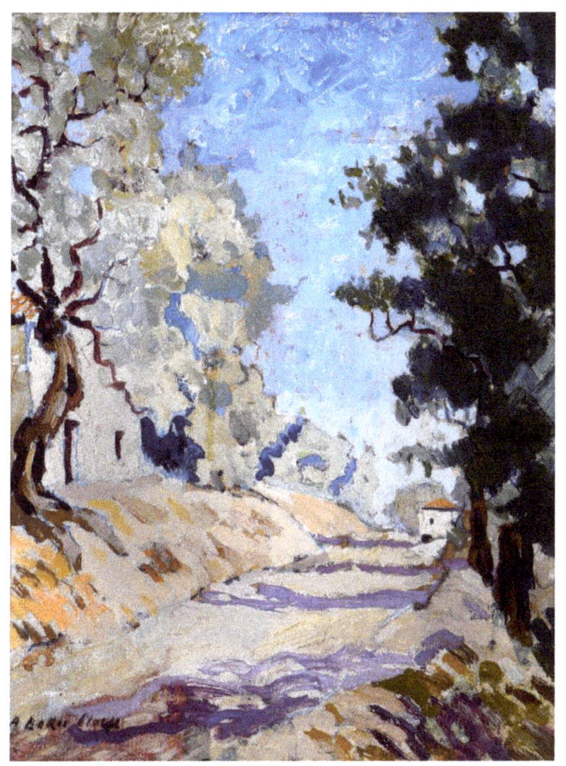

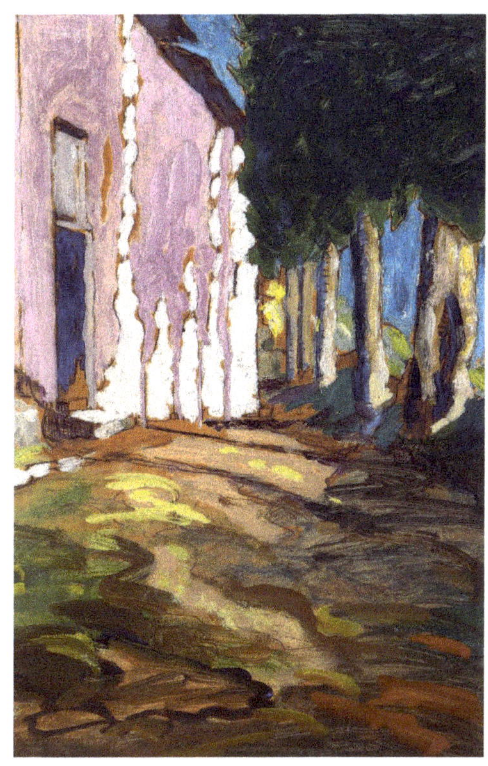

Arthur Baker Clack: *French Landscape* (above); *Tree Shadows* (right) and below: *Untitled* (French Provincial Church), courtesy Lawsons.

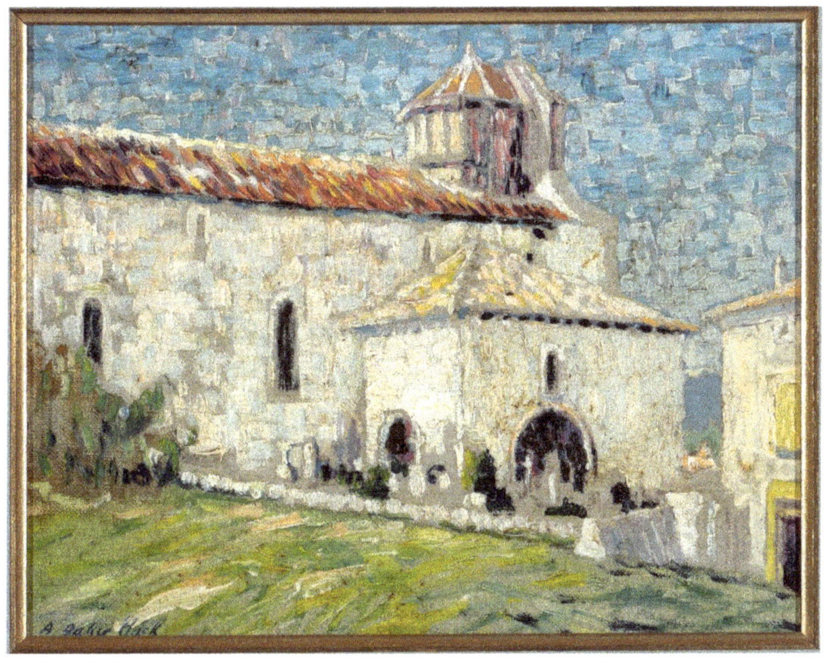

RUPERT BUNNY

Rupert Bunny gained his fame in Europe before being recognised as a leading figure of Australian painting. He came from a comfortable and cultured family where the arts and music were part of daily life. His father was a lawyer and his mother, of German origin counted Clara Schumann among her friends. Young Rupert's childhood was fed on biblical and mythological accounts. Later the subjects of his paintings were to show the influence of this background.

Bunny had his first contact with Europe at ten when his mother accompanied him for studies in Germany and Switzerland. On returning to Melbourne, he acquired drawing and oil painting techniques. In 1884 he was in London and studied at the Calderon Art School, a preparatory school for The Royal Academy.[41]

His apprenticeship was punctuated with periods in the studios in vogue. When in Paris, Jean-Paul Laurens, history painter, author of mural decorations and designs for tapestries, taught Bunny the strictness of design and colour nuance. In Bunny's view, Laurens was the most important influence in his formation. He then, widened his eclecticism with Benjamin-Constant, an orientalist, and frequented the studio of Albert Glaize, another history painter. Thus, Bunny gained skills in anatomical drawing and portraiture, skills enhanced with talent for colour. In contrast to his masters who rendered works almost in photographic art form, Bunny opted for a style which was more allusive, richer in nuance, and impressionist.

In Paris he encountered other Australian painters who had made the voyage to Europe: E. Phillips Fox arrived in May 1887, John Longstaff in September of the same year and also Tudor St George Tucker, James Quinn and the Rae sisters. At 18 bis, Impasse du Maine, the American, Max Bohm[42] was a neighbour. Now occupied by the Musée Bourdelle, it was at the time a place bustling with students in search of honours and recognition. In the street one could meet Jean-Paul Laurens, the elegant Carolus-Duran or the sculptor Jules Dalou. And Bunny "[would] speak French with an excellent English accent which gives everything he says the charm of a translation - at times unsure."[43]

In 1895, Bunny moved to avenue de Saxe and began a privileged friendship with Augustus Koopman. Together they worked on monotypes and it is difficult to say who influenced who, so alike were their results. At first Bunny produced works in black and white and in *The Reaper* where Death touches the sleeping philosopher on the shoulder, the sombre atmosphere suggests the works of Alphonse Legros.[44] The rapid execution necessary in monotypes, gives them an undeniable impression of instantaneous creation and freshness.

The monotype in colour, Nymphs in the Clearing is treated with a range of warm tones which will later come out in his Provencial works. If the influence of Koopman is to be found in Bunny, it is certainly via his monotypes. His woman in *Summer Dance*, evokes the *Danseuse, Les bras leves*, by Koopman: the contortions, the play and movement of the garment, the elongation of the silhouettes, all suggest a comparison. Yet, one can still find specific Australian touches in the background foliage in Bunny's work.

Like Eugène Boudin, Bunny travelled frequently, visiting Brittany, Véndee and Provence. He was not however a painter of skies, but that of elegant women in summer clothes, or biblical or mythological compositions. It is difficult to follow his goings and comings along the Channel coasts, especially since the reporters - and even the artist himself, used the word "Brittany" to name the coast from Pont-Aven to Boulogne-sur-Mer: seen with Australian eyes a very small territory indeed!

In his period at avenue de Saxe, Bunny met a young Beaux-Arts student, Jeanne Morel, nine years his junior, with whom he fell in love. This young girl full of distinction and grace came from a modest background. Her mother was a servant and her father a naval officer. She studied at an orphanage - Orphelinat des Arts, rue de Vanves, Paris. In 1895 and 1896 she exhibited some tapestries in a definite Art Nouveau style, and a few paintings. [45] She was also Bunny's model for *The Golden Age, Jeanne and her Terrier* and *The Muslin Dress*. After living together for some time, Bunny married Jeanne in London in 1902. Augustus Koopman and his wife were their witnesses. They returned to Etaples for the summer, the young couple taking accommodation at the Hotel Ioos.

With rapid sketches of port activities, details of a boat, a gesture, notes taken on the south bank of the Canche, some pastures in the foreground, the river and line of houses in the background, Bunny filled his sketchbooks.[46] However, unlike Koopman, he showed no true interest in the maritime life of Etaples in his work. His interest seems to have been but a matter of fortuitous circumstances due to the presence of Koopman in Etaples, and although he did a few portraits of female peasants, Bunny was not enticed to paint fishermen's wives or fishmongers: "It is so delightful here! I am hard at work and in full swing. The fishwomen are awfully picturesque though it is impossible to get near them to work: they are so rude. Their clothes get wet and cling around them so fine! I have been inland towards Montreuil, walking most wonderfully across a beautiful country. The peasants are more polite and friendly and it is easier to work. I am enjoying it so very much."[47]

When Bunny returned to Picardy in 1907, he no longer stayed in Etaples. Tired of the picturesque, he established himself in Paris-Plage, the new and fashionable seaside resort on the south bank of the Canche. Bunny had already become famous and, as early as 1904, the French Government had bought his Après le Bain far the Musée du Luxembourg. Bunny could now live comfortably and mix with people of his taste. At Paris-Plage he kept himself away from the noisy group of Etaples painters who, according to him, spent their time talking and drinking and did not work. In Etaples, Bunny had sketched the port; in Paris-Plage, he lingered on the seats of the public gardens where he could observe idle and elegant women surrounded by numerous servants. And though one of his sketchbook mentions "Les Fougères - Etaples," the villa was in Paris-Plage, at the corner of rue de Paris and rue St Alphonse. [48] The house still stands - a little changed but in the same style, with a view to the sea and the sunsets from the first floor balcony; and it is not just the grand hangings then in fashion which give certain paintings a familiar air. Among them, a model: Jeanne forever present - it would be vain to identify the works where she is the sole subject, they being numerous enough to glorify her.

Because he developed his own, many and diverse styles, it is difficult to link Bunny to any precise one. His training in London put him in touch with the pre-Raphaelites and Symbolists, of which Arnold Bocklin and Pierre Puvis de Chavannes were, for him, the most notable figures. In France, his training was more academic. When the "isms" competed for entry to the galleries, it was impressionism and "plein-airisme" which, obviously, drew him. But his, was an impressionism wisely tempered and well controlled. Bunny, unlike his compatriot, John Peter Russell, did not follow Claude Monet. "He was eclectic," mentions Colette Reddin.[49] He also had many affinities with the American painters he knew in Paris - Richard Miller, Max Bohm and Augustus Koopman. And even if he "borrowed" Pierre Bonnard's palette for his landscapes of the South of France and his mythological scenes, Bunny did not lose his soul: he stayed himself, he continued to enrich his technique, and he remained inimitable.

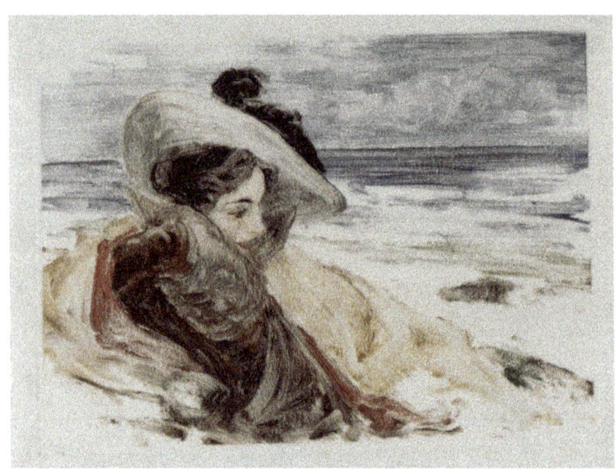

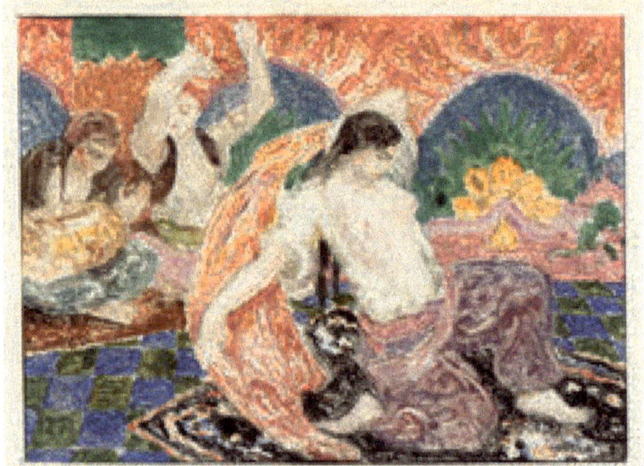

Monotype is the process in which the artist works directly on the metal or glass plate with printer's ink or paint. The plate is printed on paper, usually only once.

Bunny regularly practiced this technique. In 1921 he exhibited 100 monotypes of mythological subjects at the Galerie Georges Petit in Paris. Artists of the period were very enthusiastic about monotypes. Edgar Degas, who considered himself as the "re-discoverer" of the technique, held it in high esteem and contributed to its popularity and fame. Around 1880, he produced fifty or so monotypes entitled: *Scenes de Bordel.* Prendergast, an American painter, used the process in a series of work between 1895 and 1901; his models had many affinities with those painted by Bunny. [50]

Rupert Bunny: *By the Sea* (above).

Rupert Bunny: *Eastern Dancer* (1921) (below).

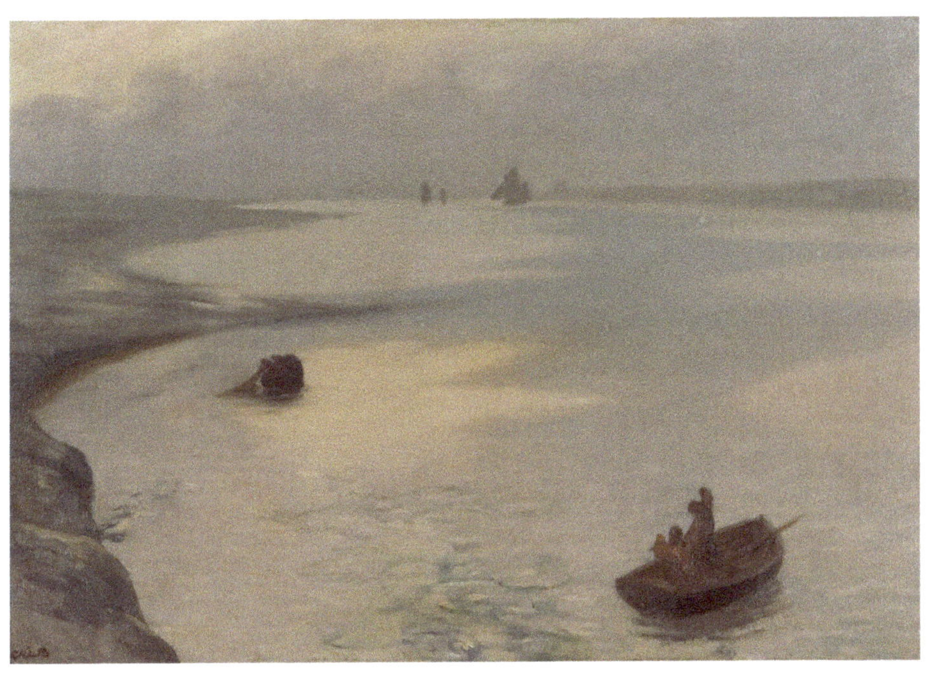

Rupert Bunny: *La Canche a Etaples.*

In Bunny's Etaples landscapes, the Canche plays an inspiring role. In *Le Pont d'Etaples,* Louise Koopman and Jeanne Morel are looking at a child.[51] The work is delicate yet boldly and swiftly drawn - a "pochade." In *La Canche a Etaples,* the river stretches to its mouth in a view with a Japanese touch; the boats fade into an iridescent atmosphere in monochrome, with the Canche shimmering in the full moon. It finally threads its way through the prairies and meadows of Enocq and Beutin in *Près d'Etaples.* These landscapes, showing the River Canche, painted somewhat from above, remind us of the work done by Fries Thaulow at Montreuil-sur-Mer.[52]

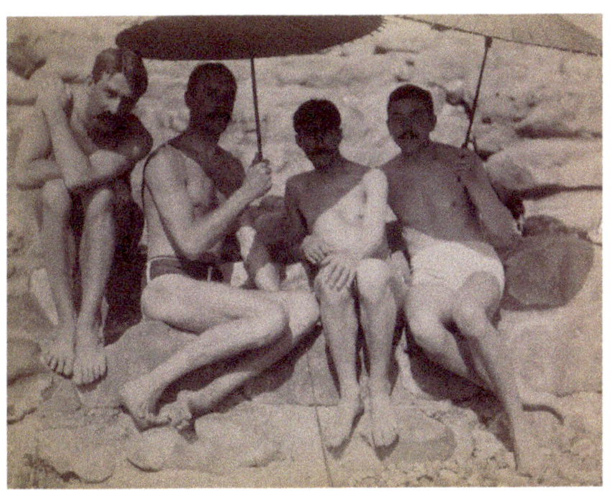

Rupert Bunny and friends on the beach, 1903.

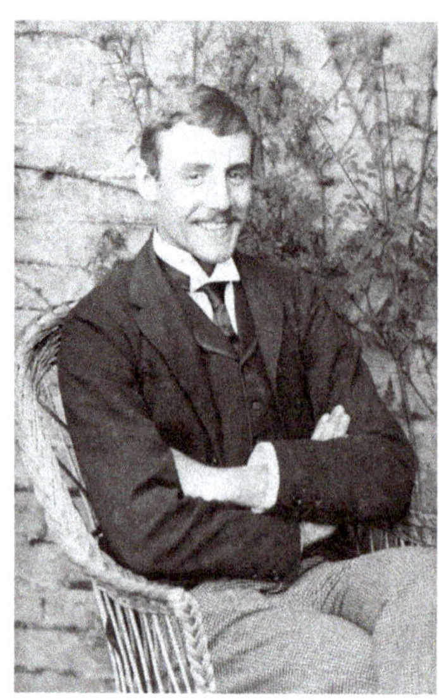

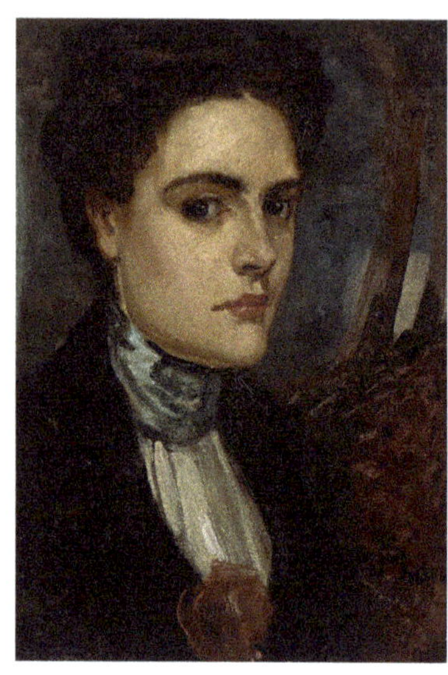

Rupert Bunny in Provence 1884. His *Portrait of Jeanne Morel,* 1901.

The painting *Deux Femmes nues sur une plage* seems contemporary to *Femme lisant sur la plage.* On observing the range of colours, the black rocks in the foreground, one has the impression that the artist used the same setting, a small fishing beach north of Etaples: Equihen. It was also in Equihen that Koopman painted his *Baigneurs* with a fine sensuality of colours. While Bunny increased his colour range and participated in the 1904 Salon d'Automne, Fauvism was in the air...

Rupert Bunny: *Femme lisant sur la plage.*

A woman is sitting on the edge of a cliff holding a book; below her, the sea spreads around a bay. On the black rocks, people are shell fishing. The scene is painted in subdued tones, modelled in browns and yellows. The sombre rocks frame the silhouette of the reader. The colours bring to mind works painted in 1902 and 1907. The setting is probably once more Equihen where Koopman and Max Bohm and their wives and children resided in summer.

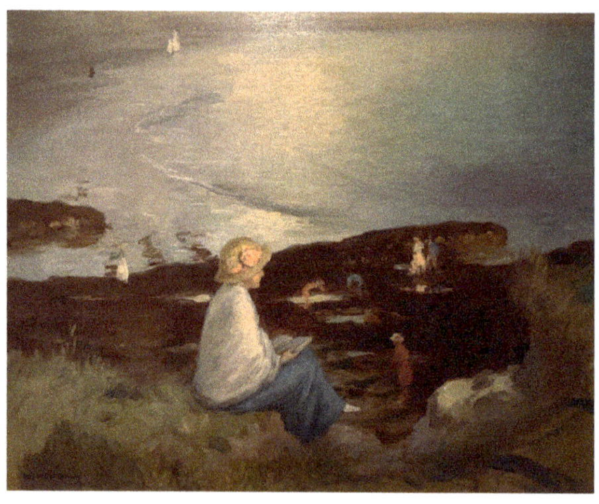

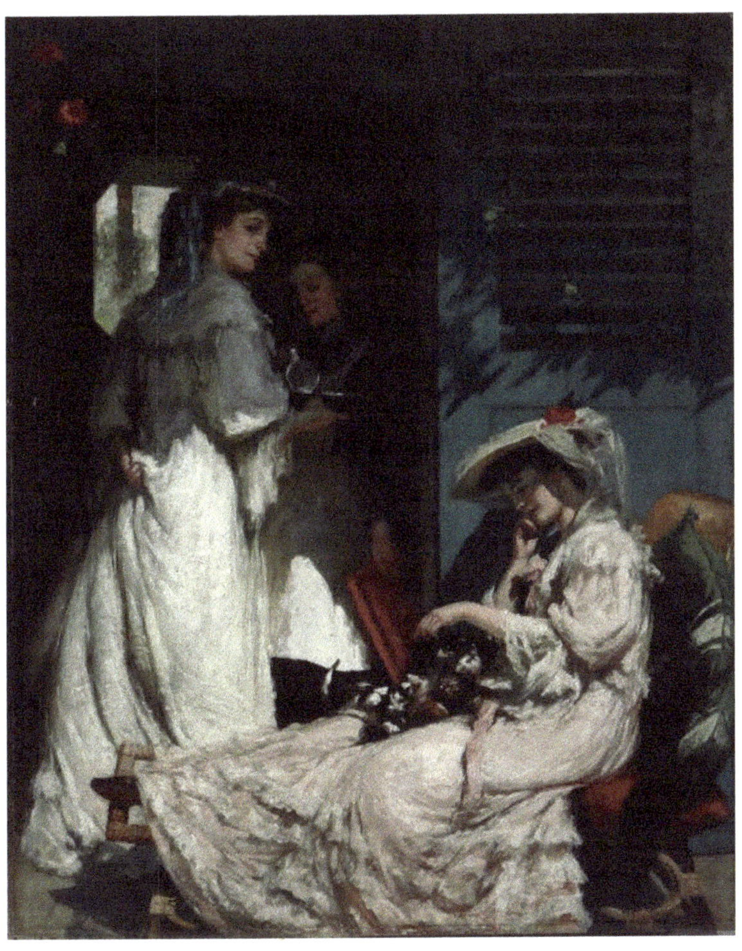

Rupert Bunny: *Summer Morning.*

Bunny had his first idea of *Summer Morning* in Paris-Plage: his 1907 sketchbook gives evidence of the fact with drawings of the kittens, the jug, Jeanne, and the servant.

In the preparatory work, everything is already placed: the shaded area from where the visitor and the servant emerge, the sunny area where a woman (Jeanne) reclines on a chaise-longue with kittens on her lap. Light and subjects placed, the brush has not yet defined the important presence of the dresses: here they are only masses hardly completed. The dresses in the final version are lengthened by rows of lace hanging heavily to the floor, which when walking are held by a hand, to the great satisfaction of Bunny for whom dresses symbolise "women", and which he revelled in painting in the series *Days and Nights in August*, between 1907 and 1911. Therefore, when the critic of *Le Figaro*, commented that the artist "admirably gifted, had let himself go so far as to produce too much, without discretion or diversity,"[53] Bunny explained: "When women began to wear short skirts, I no longer wished to paint them."[54]

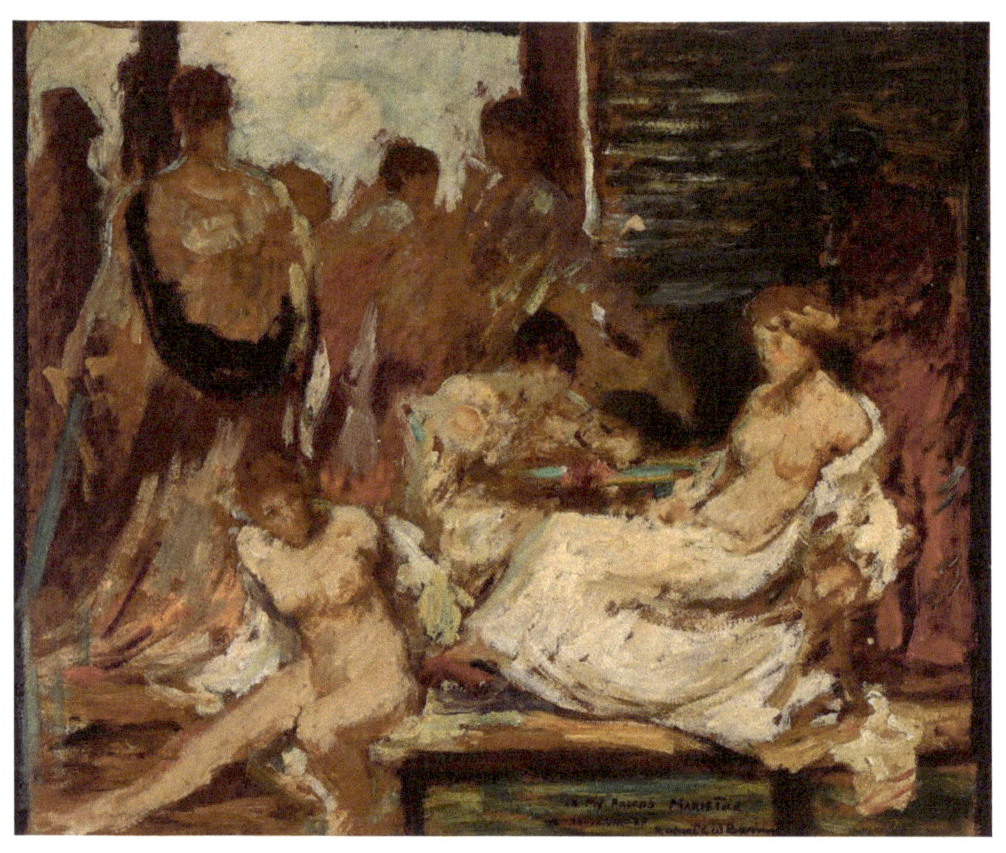

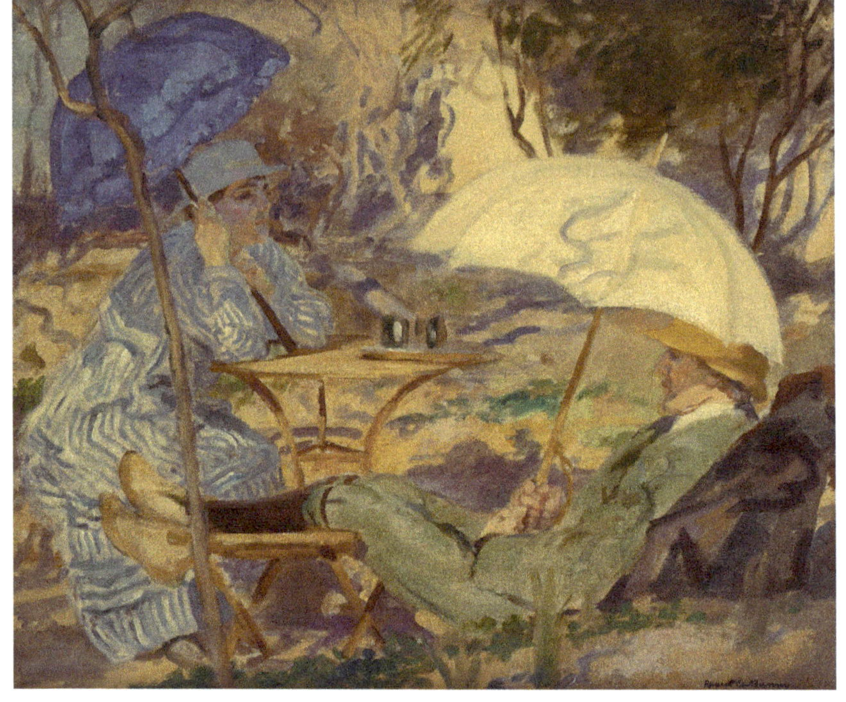

Rupert Bunny: *Study for Summer Time,* 1907 "for Marie Tuck."

Rupert Bunny: *Cavalaire* (c. 1910)

ISOBEL RAE

Isobel Rae was born into a family of five children,[55] in Collingwood, a Melbourne suburb. Her father, Thomas Rae, was in the soap manufacturing business; her mother, Janet Love, of Scottish origin, was pleased to see her two last daughters, Alison and Isobel, become interested in painting: she was herself a portrait painter[56] and exhibited at the Victorian Academy of Arts in Melbourne. In 1877, Isobel entered the School of Fine Arts of the National Gallery of Victoria. She met Rupert Bunny and John Longstaff and worked under the direction of George Frederick Folingsby, who held classes in life drawing with models. Her competitive training made the young girl a skilful artist at sketching people and her studies, completed in 1887, were crowned with success.[57] The same year, Janet and her two daughters, Alison and Isobel, left for Europe. Thomas Rae did not make the voyage andwasnevermentionedlater.

The early works done by Iso Rae in Australia belong to a very particular atmosphere: her children standing on the edge of woods evoke "the lost child" - a subject special to Australian painting. It contrasts a child's innocence with the hostility of the Australian bush. Frederick McCubbin illustrated the theme in paintings with short but significant titles: *Lost and Found.*[58] Australian works by Isobel such as *Child near the Woods* or *Little Girl in the Woods*, find their extension in *Pierrot* and *Femme au Jardin*, both painted in Picardy.

On arrival in Paris in August 1887, the three women looked for lodgings, settled themselves and met with other Australians there: Rupert Bunny of course but also Tudor St George Tucker and E. Phillips Fox. They enrolled at the Académie Colarossi, avenue Victor Hugo. The professors at the time were Courtois and Dagnan-Bouveret[59] - the later being the most influential in Isobel's training. Dagnan-Bouveret worked along the lines of Bastien-Lepage[60] - that of rural realism of the time and his *Chevaux à l'abreuvoir*, shows this to an extent which surprises even today, not only in the photographic result, but also in the detail of the manes and harnesses.

Isobel worked passionately with the Salon in view. Alison, who had a gift for writing, served as a correspondent for Australian magazines and wrote in detail of student life in Paris - their hopes and their deceptions.[61] When the lights of the Salon were extinguished, the academies released their students and the Rae family decided they would spend the summer in Etaples at Mme Pannier's: "According to the postcard they sent me, the Raes are again in Etaples," Max Bohm wrote to his mother during summer 1890.[62] Around 1893 mother and daughters finally installed themselves in Etaples, lodging at 3 rue des Violiers - a calm street away from the Grand-Place, not far from the Hotel Ioos and where, at the back of a garden, they occupied accommodation offered by Dr Dacquet. In gratitude, Isobel drew a portrait of Mme Dacquet.

In Etaples, Iso Rae observed the local population and the rites of a community: the market, the processions, funerals and other blessings. Her paintings as well as her drawings, show a strong influence of the surroundings, a connivance in which humour, if not caricature, has its place. Nothing pleased her more than to find herself amongst *Les Acheteuses* (market customers) in order to seize the various attitudes and the facial characteristics and expressions. This constant reference to reality comes from her professor, Dagnan-Bouveret who stated: "We need to feel the earth under our feet and those amongst us who do abstractions without the support of a serious study of reality are nearly always wrong."[63] It is also with amusement that Iso Rae looks at *Le Garde Champêtre* (local policeman), a rapidly executed drawing in pastel.

All in all, Isobel and Alison Rae spent half a century in Etaples and integrated well with the local people. But with the escalation of the war in 1915, the exhibitions held in Le Touquet ceased. On 6 August 1916, Janet Love, their mother, died of illness and was buried at Le Touquet. Dr Dacquet also passed away in that year. The majority of artists fled. The flow of injured soldiers was such that in Le Touquet, the hotels - the Savoy, the Hermitage and the Nouveau Casino, were requisitioned and transformed into hospitals. Alison and Isobel volunteered to give help and comfort during those barbaric times: Alison was employed at the military hospitals, while Isobel worked in the YMCA supply stores,[64] as well as in the Etaples Camp on the northern side of the railway station where she sketched scenes of the day-to-day life of the soldiers. When Dr Dacquet's studio was destroyed by the bombing, the sisters took temporary lodgings with Mlle Geneau, in rue du Rivage. They left this address for 14 rue d'Hérambault, before finally leaving for England in 1934 - but Isobel, nostalgic for the place and the friends she had left behind, wrote to Achille Caron, her painting supplier:

Dear Achille, [65]
What must you be thinking of me to not have acknowledged your postcard and the article "Etaples," the work of your son Achille? But as you can see by this letter, we changed address just a week ago and since I have not stopped. Today I feel better although still weak and I do not want to delay my reply any longer. It must be a great pleasure to have in your midst, a writer who is already so famous. All he has written on this particular subject expresses well the melancholy and charm of the Etaples neighbourhood. Congratulate him sincerely on our behalf and, at the same time, wish him good luck for the book that he has undertaken.

Our best wishes to you and yours,

Iso Rae

Before her departure, Isobel donated a few works to the Musée du Touquet, among which were two huge "processions" - the quality of which have not altered a scrap since their installation.

Iso Rae's first work located in Etaples, *The Chicken Trader*, is dated 1888, a short time after the family's arrival. The scene, setin a kitchen, shows a trader and a middle-aged woman in discussion. According to Alison (Iso's sister), we are chez Mme Pannier, "A little old, grey-haired lady who was certainly good looking in her youth as she is still pretty at sixty two." In the light of what we know of the work of Isobel Rae, the anecdotal side of this painting rather surprises. It is her "beginning" and a piece of evidence left behind on the successful path followed by the gifted artist. Mme Pannier ought to have been flattered to find herself represented larger than life in a painting which, after leaving France, went around the world as far as Dunedin.[66]

Iso Rae's work in pastels is far from the tonal paintings of her early years. Already present in *The Blacksmith's Forge*, this tendency definitely takes hold in *Procession à Etaples* and its subtle harmonies of yellows, blacks and pinks. The painting depicts a group of elderly men in black, singing hymns. In the foreground at left, young girls in yellow dresses contrast with the dense black of the suits. On the right, a mother watching the procession carries an infant in her arms; next to her a little girl, wearing a hat, looks towards us. All the elements fit in perfectly in this close-up with the participants as a frieze. Considering that processions were a rather fashionable theme at the turn of the 19th c.,[67] it is obvious that hers gives evidence of her creative imagination.

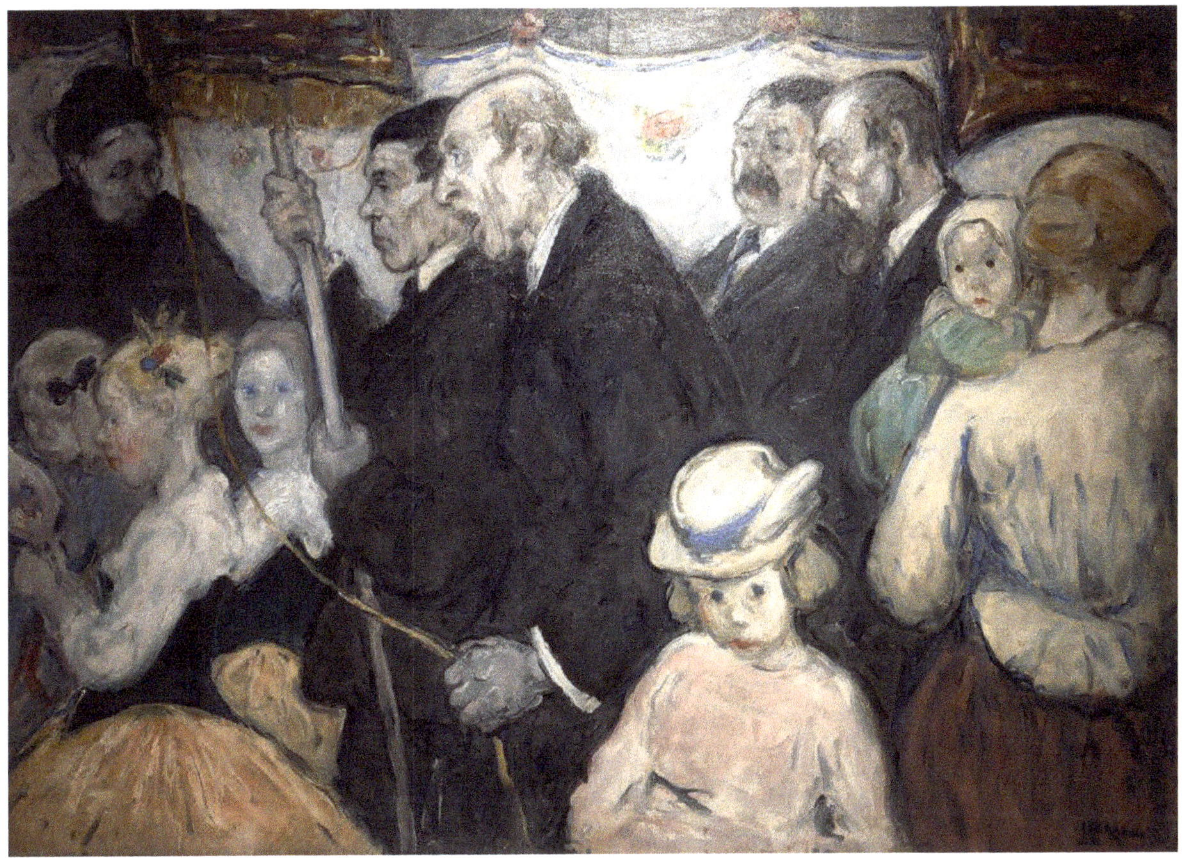

Isobel Rae: La Procession à Etaples, Musée du Touquet.

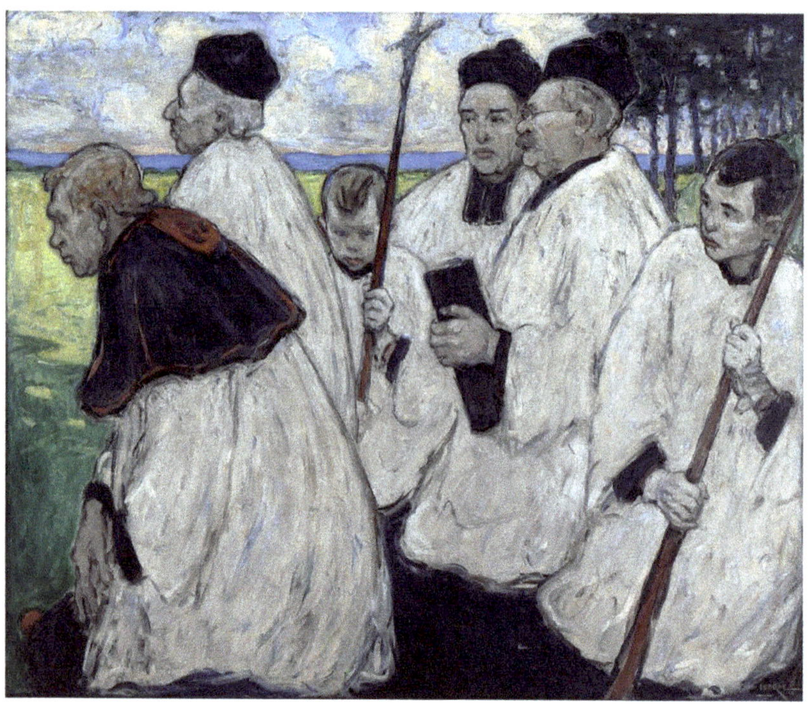

Isobel Rae: *Les Rogations*, Musée du Touquet.

The artist repeats the setting of the Procession à Etaples with priests in surplice and caps, accompanied by choir boys. The oblique lines of the large crosses, the placing of the group in an open semicircle draws not only one's attention, but also makes one part of the scene. The turbulent clouds, the far off sea, the trees, the yellow fields of ripe wheat make it a country scene in summer.

In the catholic religion, the "Rogations" were solemn processions which took place "on the three days preceding Ascension, to ask God to bless the harvests, at which time litanies of the Saints are chanted."[68]

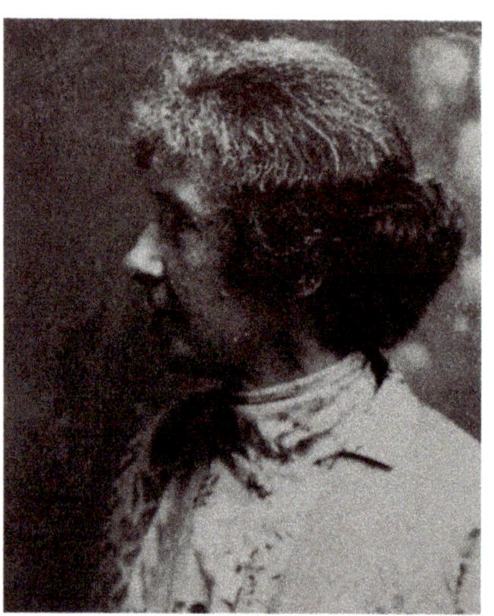

Iso Rae.

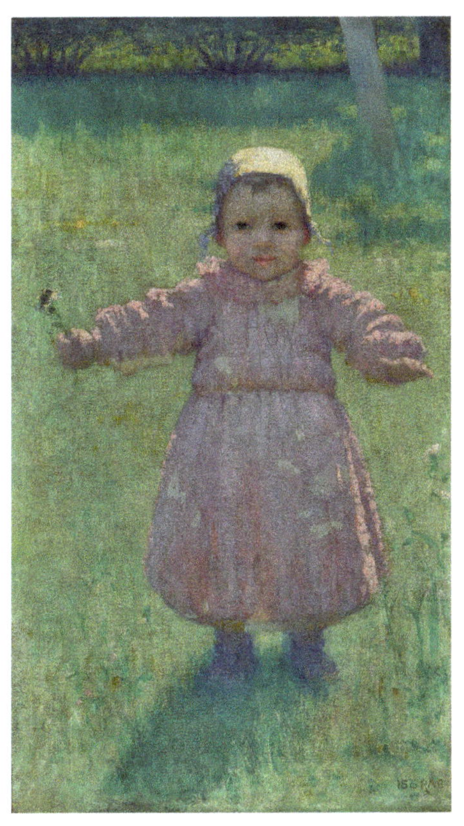

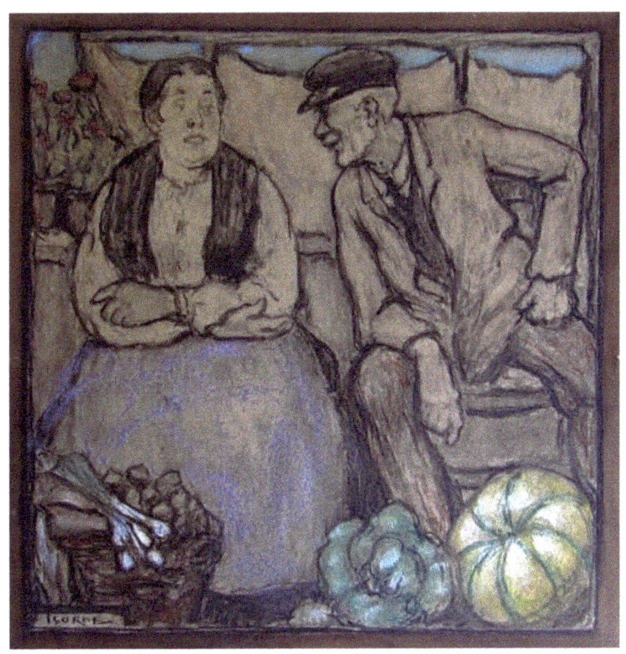

Isobel Rae: *Young Girl, Etaples*, 1892.

Isobel Rae: *The Joker*,
wash and crayon on brown paper,
c1913,
courtesy 69 John Street.

Isobel Rae: *Portrait of a Young Girl.*

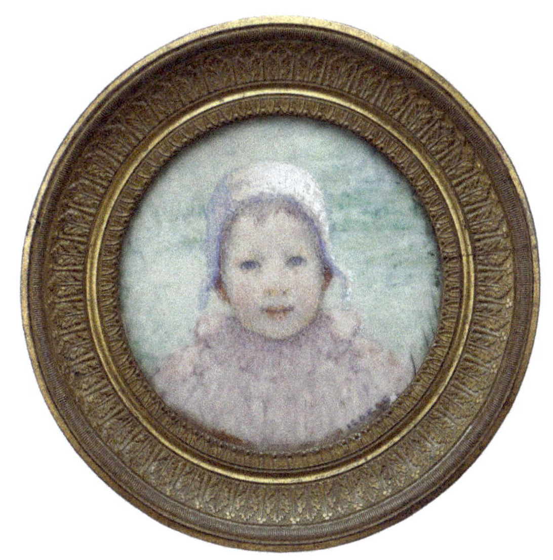

ALISON RAE

Alison Rae's[69] artistic career cannot be compared to that of her younger sister. However, her identity card mentions her profession as "artist." She received art training in Melbourne before going to France. She painted still-lifes which she exhibited at the Salon with Isobel.

Alison put her brushes aside for the pen, but, not quite content with writing picturesque chronicles about the artistic life in Etaples, she launched into writing fiction and "My Pretty Moira" was published in *The Gentleman's Magazine,* London.[70]

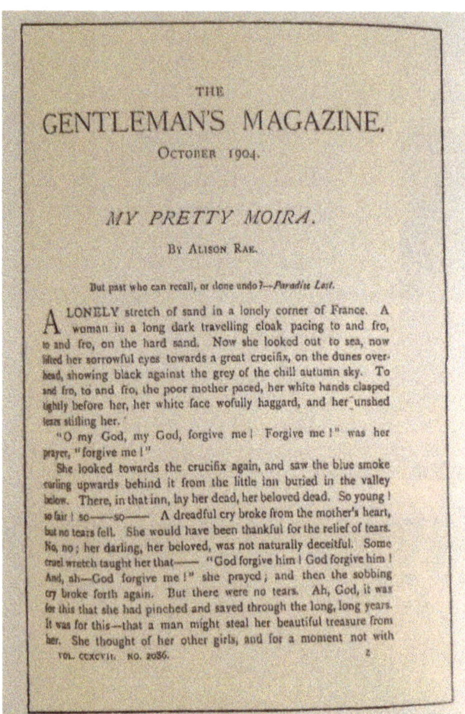

THE

GENTLEMAN'S MAGAZINE.

OCTOBER 1904.

MY PRETTY MOIRA.

BY ALISON RAE.

But past who can recall, or done undo?—*Paradise Lost.*

A LONELY stretch of sand in a lonely corner of France. A woman in a long dark travelling cloak pacing to and fro, to and fro, on the hard sand. Now she looked out to sea, now lifted her sorrowful eyes towards a great crucifix, on the dunes overhead, showing black against the grey of the chill autumn sky. To and fro, to and fro, the poor mother paced, her white hands clasped tightly before her, her white face wofully haggard, and her unshed tears stifling her.

"O my God, my God, forgive me! Forgive me!" was her prayer, "forgive me!"

She looked towards the crucifix again, and saw the blue smoke curling upwards behind it from the little inn buried in the valley below. There, in that inn, lay her dead, her beloved dead. So young! so fair! so—so— A dreadful cry broke from the mother's heart, but no tears fell. She would have been thankful for the relief of tears. No, no; her darling, her beloved, was not naturally deceitful. Some cruel wretch taught her that— "God forgive him! God forgive him! And, ah—God forgive me!" she prayed; and then the sobbing cry broke forth again. But there were no tears. Ah, God, it was for this that she had pinched and saved through the long, long years. It was for this—that a man might steal her beautiful treasure from her. She thought of her other girls, and for a moment not with

VOL. CCXCVII. NO. 2086. 2

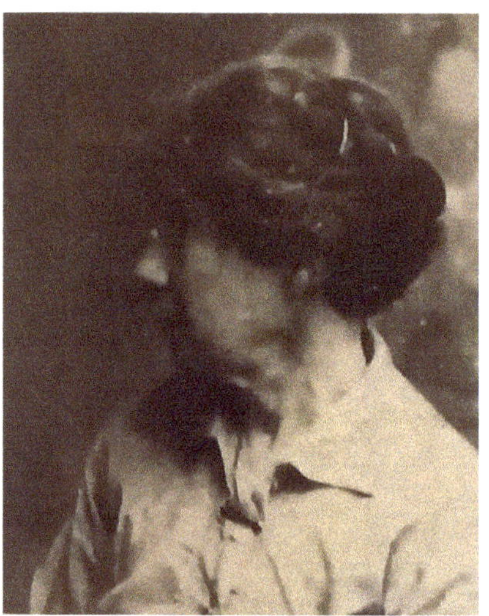

Alison Rae.

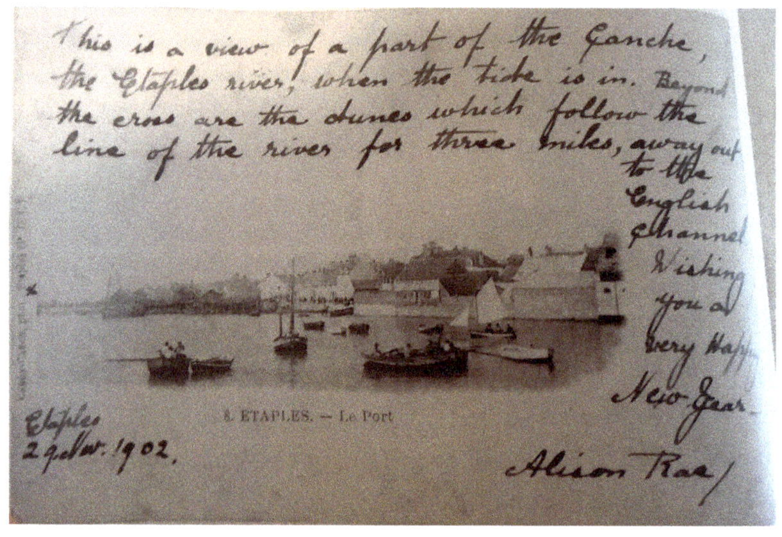

HILDA RIX NICHOLAS

Hilda Rix grew up in a favourable artistic atmosphere: her mother, Elisabeth, was a painter and participated in Melbourne exhibitions. From 1902 to 1905, Hilda studied drawing at the National Gallery School of Design which Frederick McCubbin ran with kind authority. She exhibited at the Victorian Artists' Society. Arthur Streeton, a friend of the family, suggested that Hilda should be sent to Paris to complete her artistic education. Shortly after the death of her father, Hilda, her sister Elsie, and her mother, left for Europe.

In 1907 they spent spring and summer in London. Hilda studied with artist, John Hassal. By autumn, the family were in Paris and Hilda frequented the academies. However, anxious to retain her own personality and style, she often changed masters: "If you are wise, and if you have originality, do not stay too long at any one of these schools, but take what good you can from any or all; then if you can, rent your own studio and work out your own salvation, making sure first that your drawing will stand the test of any circumstance." For the first time she tries a tricky technique: oil painting and takes the advice of Monsieur Delécluse, "whose colour is too drab to carry one far, but whose excellent corrections on drawing make a splendid foundation."[71]

Spring 1908: the young woman, eager to discover new horizons, left her studio rue Bara on the Left Bank for the Midi, Italy and Switzerland. Upon her return to Paris, she enrolled at the Académie Colarossi which she left for the Académie de la Grande Chaumière[72] where she worked with Steinlen. She developed her gift for drawing which she was to use in Etaples and later in Morocco. An American painter, Richard Miller,[73] gave her a few lessons in composition. Her time under his tuition was of more consequence than Hilda cared to admit. She borrowed his subjects - portraits of young and idle women, as well as his titles: *The Chinese Dress* and *The Mirror*.

In July 1910, she went to Etaples for the first time, "to spend summer there," she said. Hilda arrived in a rainy and muddy town but its charm was such that she stayed for the rest of the year and rented one of Mme Pannier's studios.

A neighbour, Jules Adler,[74] took interest in the young artist and Hilda accepted his advice with gratitude, conscious that she should make the most of comments she would have had to pay highly for in Paris. In the colony of artists, Hilda mixed with Americans and English and became a respected and influential member. This was not surprising to those who knew her good humour, her enterprising spirit and sociability. Henry Ossawa Tanner and Harry Van der Weyden, Arthur Baker Clack, and an Englishman, Gwilt Jolley, were her close friends.

Hilda Rix painted few landscapes in Etaples and obviously preferred "women" subjects. Isobel Rae who had been in Etaples for some twenty years, showed her how to proceed to sketch the locals: a cursive line, both sympathetic yet implacable with Daumier as a reference. In her works, female models are omnipresent in all states and all conditions. First it is her landlady in *Madame*

Monthuys-Pannier then, the housewives in blue aprons and headgear typical of Etaples in *Au travail.* The market gave Hilda varied observation facilities: market women, groups of gossiping housewives and peasants: all made up the settings for her sketches which she composed spontaneously on the spot. But not only everyday subjects: elegant and languid women pose in *Pink Scarf* or *The Blue Dress*, a mother dreams of her son sent to the Front in *A Mother of France.* And still another feminine subject, taken from I know not what Middle Age fable stands, dressed up, in *Return from the Hunt.* Hilda loved costumes whether they were from yester-year or today, from Europe or the Orient. So as to mitigate the impatience of her models, not always dressed to their liking, she would take photographs for her large compositions on canvas. It was not until Morocco that a masculine element appeared in her work.

Aside from portraits of young women, Hilda would sketch during walks: the old houses, the cobbled streets and the pig market in the square when visiting Harry Van der Weyden in Montreuil. Coloured pencil sketches or large oils on canvas expressed, via a figurative tradition, a remarkable ability as a colourist. However, nothing exaggerated, just a few expressionist tendencies - a faint echo of the pictorial revolution which was manifesting all over Europe.

At the beginning of February 1912, Hilda undertook a voyage to Morocco but she did not venture to go alone to a country in political unrest. At that time, Morocco was coveted by Europe and the treaties which had just been signed with France in no way established civil peace: Fez was the scene of massacres which were committed in April of the same year.

The journey was set up in Etaples by Henry Ossawa Tanner.[75] She travelled with both he and his wife, Jessie; Annie Simpson, a painter friend, accompanied them. Hilda wrote to the Van der Weydens that they were visiting Madrid and Toledo where they admired Greco and Velasquez; then they stopped in Cordoba and Algésiras. On 4 February, they were in Gibraltar. Carried away by the exaltation due to the revelation of a new territory, she penned comparisons proper to other painter-travellers: Eugène Delacroix had written of "the antique world in the streets," whereas Hilda met "Moors out of a biblical episode."[76]

In Tangier, they stayed at the Hotel de France, where European visitors would usually stop. Did she, by chance, meet Henri Matisse there? - He was in Tangier, at the same hotel from 29 January to mid-April.

The drawings done in coloured pencils - a quick means of capturing the multiple attractions in the street - show great control of execution. Hilda learnt a lot in Morocco and the stay marked a turning point in her work. *Young Arab Boy, Market in Tangier, Couple de Marocains (A Couple of Moroccans)*, are accomplished works. Upon her return, Hilda was sufficiently satisfied with her works to exhibit them in Paris. The French State bought her *Grand Marché à Tanger (Main Market in Tangier)* for the Musee du Luxembourg, to the great pride of the artist whose talent was then recognised.

She returned to Morocco the following year but this time, in the company of her sister, Elsie. She found herself back in the cities which had enchanted her, and renewed with her "beloved Arabs." In 1913 and 1914, she participated in the Salon des Peintres Orientalistes Français: "Miss Rix's Moroccan sketches show an agile and intelligent execution. In a stroke she captures gestures and facial expressions, as well as the draperies and folds of the clothing. Her crowds of Arabs are expressive, typically characteristic, drawn with firmness. Picturesque vignettes without being anecdotal. Charming debut, very promising..." wrote Louis Vauxcelles.[77]

When the war broke out, the three women hurriedly left France for England, leaving their work behind with Mme Cresson. Harry Van der Weyden helpfully managed to save most of it. Aboard the ship, Elsie and her mother caught typhoid fever. Elsie died in September 1914 and her mother in March 1916, their deaths being followed by another episode equally tragic. Major George Matson Nicholas, passing through Etaples, was attracted to paintings he saw in a deserted studio. Enquiring of the painter, he eventually met Hilda and fell under her spell. They were married in London in October 1916 and after a short honeymoon, George returned to the Front. He was killed in the November.[78] So many painful experiences profoundly affected Hilda's morale. Works of the period show evidence of the personal crisis she was suffering. *A Mother of France* shows an aged woman seated in an Etaples interior, gazing into space - an image of all mothers waiting for bad news.

Once the war was over, Hilda returned to Australia and exhibited her Picardy paintings in Melbourne, then in Sydney in 1919 where they were well received: after the turmoil of the war, "Parisian" art was on its way to Australasia. Seizing the opportunity of an exhibition of her work in Paris in 1924, she returned to Europe with Dorothy Richmond. She revisited her beloved Etaples and paid a visit to Harry Van der Weyden, still living at Montreuil. She also visited Brittany and, in the vicinity of Quimper, painted the "Bigouden" surroundings.

In 1928, Hilda married Edgar Wright to whom she had a son. But she had always in mind the happy, youthful days in France, to the point where she decorated her cottage in Knockalong in the Picardian style - certainly a very surprising sight in the Australian countryside! She made her last voyage to France in 1950 but her delicate health and failing sight no longer enabled her to paint.

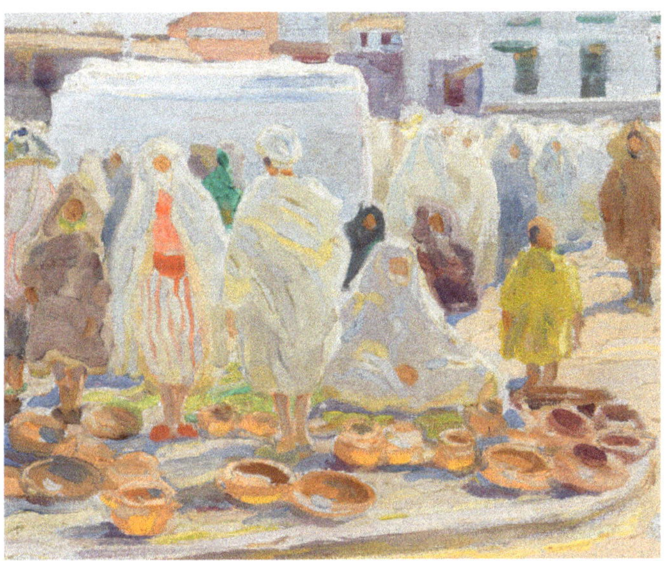

Hilda Rix: *Seller of Earthenware Pots* (1914).

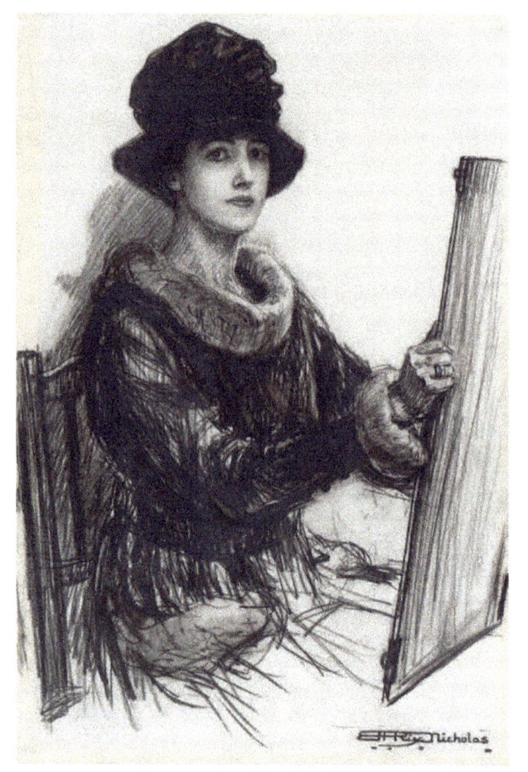

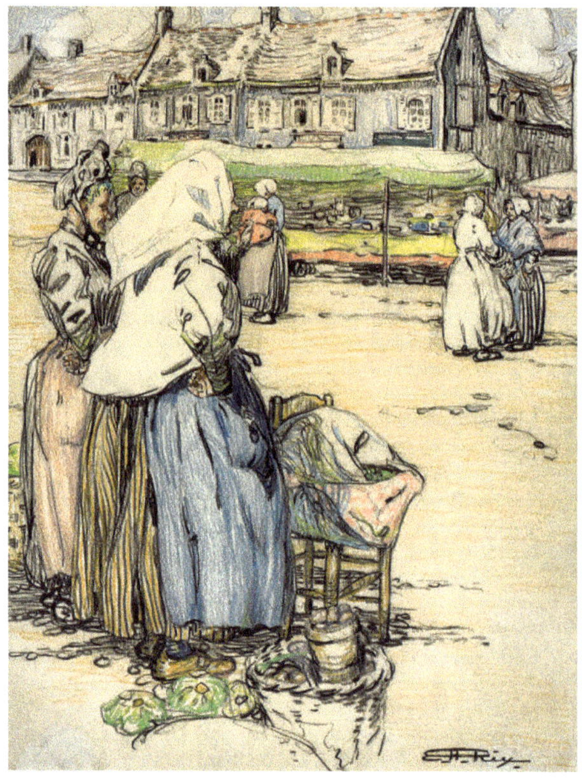

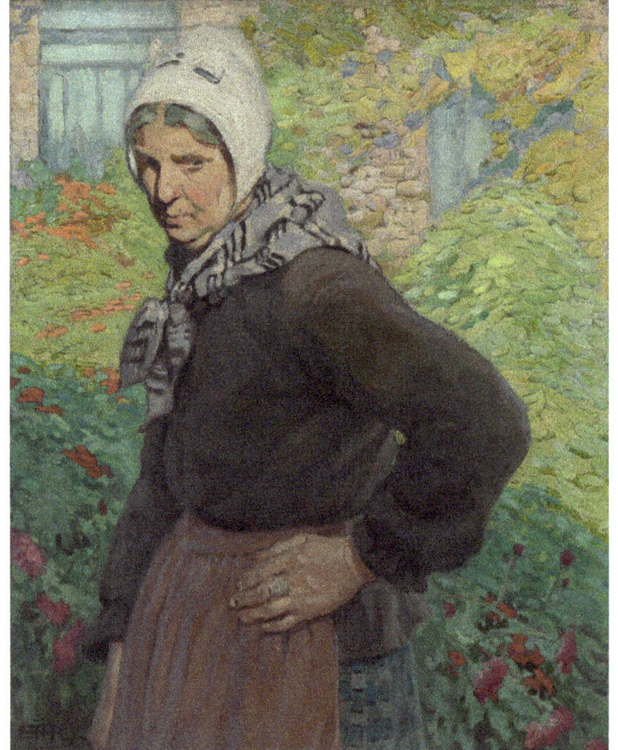

Hilda Rix Nicholas: *Self Portrait*

Hilda Rix Nicholas:
Market at Etaples (1910) (above).

Hilda Rix Nicholas:
In Picardy (1914)
National Gallery of Victoria.

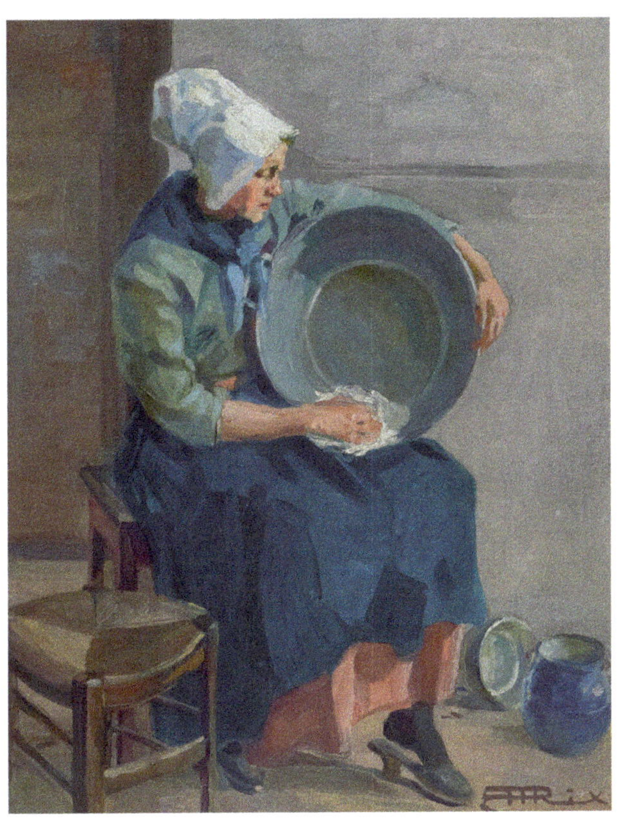

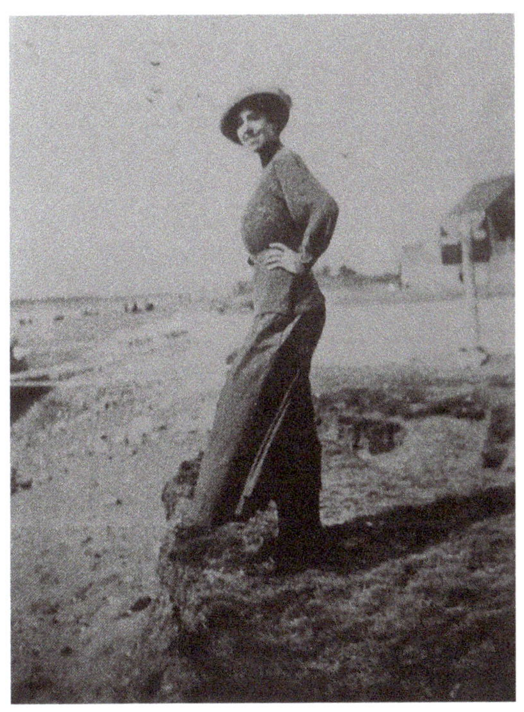

Hilda Rix Nicholas: *The Scullery Maid* (1914).

Hilda Rix Nicholas at Etaples.

Hilda Rix Nicholas: *Grand-Mere* (Art Gallery of NSW).

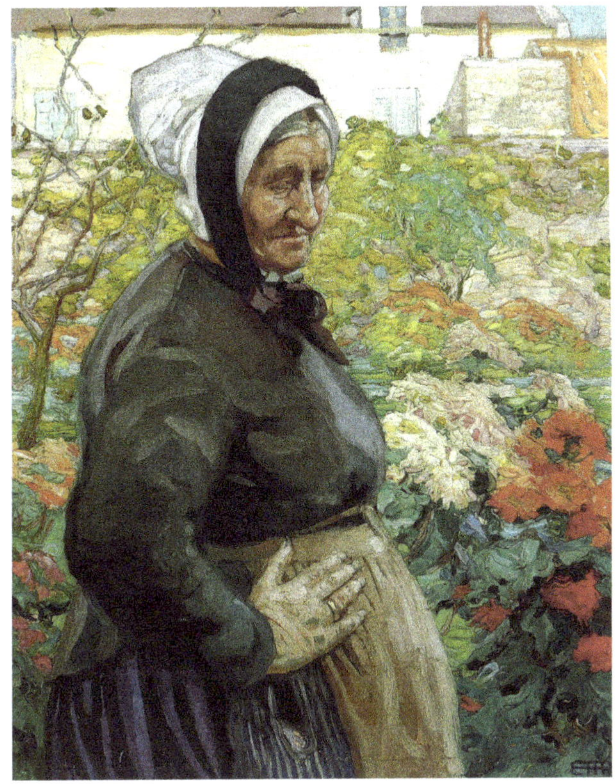

MARIE TUCK

Amongst the list of women who expressed a new trend in Australian and New Zealand painting at the beginning of the 20th c., should be specially mentioned Stella Bowen, Dorrit Black, Bessie Davidson, Margaret Preston and Kathleen O'Connor. Marie Tuck[79] must also be counted among those who, despite Victorian society prejudices, realised their artistic aspirations. She was born into a modest family of seven children, their father, Edward Tuck, being director of a private school. Marie forged an artist's career due to her strong will permitting her, more than once, to overcome hostile and impoverished conditions. Was she not, when in Adelaide at the age of twenty, a florist by day and a student in the evening? She was then studying at James Ashton's new Norwood Art School.[80] Her obstinacy saw her in Perth in 1896 when she rented a studio in Wellington Street, participated in the inaugural exhibition of the West Australian Society of Arts, and taught painting. For eight years, she had no other aim but to save the necessary funds to travel to Europe.

In 1904, she finally headed for Paris. The same year, Bessie Davidson and Margaret Preston also made the voyage and all three met in the capital. Had Marie waited too long to realise her dream? When she joined the academies, she reduced her age by six years.

She did not attend the expensive academies in Paris but lived at 55 rue de Montparnasse, a few blocks from Rupert Bunny. Taking care of Bunny's studio, she would, in return, receive lessons from the painter whom she revered. Bunny already had a good reputation and his talent had been noted in numerous Salons. From him, Marie retained a colourful palette and a softness of colour. She also owed co him her monotype ability. So much work allied to so much talent explained her rapid progress. Bunny himself was surprised and admirative: "She did in one year what I have never seen done by any other woman in five."[81] It was Bunny who advised her to leave Paris during summer. She was in Etaples in 1907 and 1908, then every year from 1910 to 1914; she also stayed in Brittany,[82] and *Bridal Preparation*, with its iridescent lighting and pink tones obtained "distinction" in the 1911 Salon.

In Etaples, Marie Tuck lived on boulevard Billiet near the quay, amongst the subjects of her paintings. Her archetype was a sailor's wife in the nearby fish market or around the water pump where the gossip was ceaseless. Marie had little in common with the young idle yet cultivated women of Bunny's works. *Ferme à Lefaux, Portail de l'Eglise de Montreuil Intérieur à Saint-Josse*[83] evoke her promenades in the surrounding countryside.

In Summer 1907 she attended the ceremony for the unveiling of statues at the Mariners' Calvary. She also worked on two large canvasses which she presented at the 1908 Salon: *Les Commeres* was remarked on by the critics for its "well planned setting," and *Le Marché aux poissons,* for "harmony of subtle and shaded tones." Marie thought it worth sending both of them to the Eleventh Federal Art Exhibition in Adelaide. The city museum purchased the *Fish Market* which, at last, enabled her to live more comfortably.

After returning to Australia in 1914, she taught drawing and painting, and introduced the nude figure at the South Australian School of Arts and Crafts in Adelaide. In her Frewville studio, she lived surrounded by students in her role as mentor and as one who had taken part in Parisian artistic life. She encouraged the young with strictness, urging them beyond their limits and taught them "how to become an artist."[84]

The unveiling of the statues at the Calvary on 15 August 1907, gave rise to an important ceremony assembling the Etaples population. The light brightens the facades of the houses, making whiter the dresses of the girls taking communion, the clergymen's surplices and the women's headgear, rendering even darker the compact mass of the worshippers around the Mariners' Calvary. Marie Tuck becomes impressionist using a rapid brush, which suggests that she did not paint in detail neither the figures nor the banners in the scene.

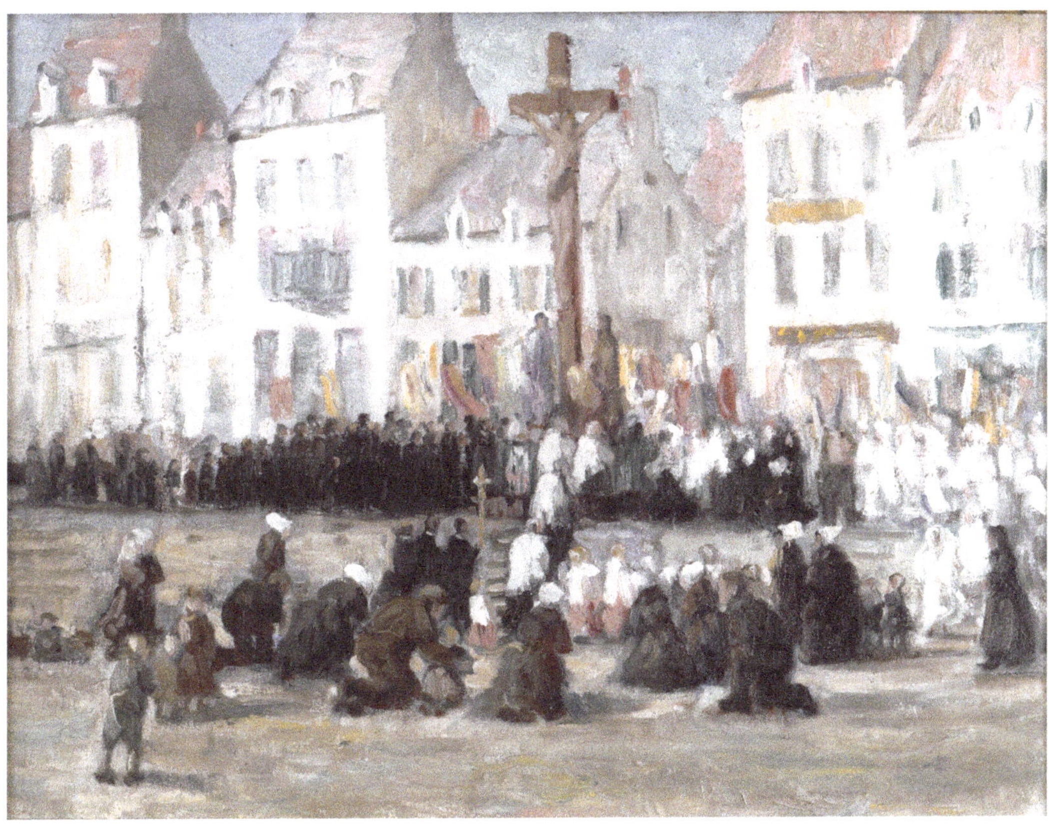

Marie Tuck: *Procession of 15 August at Etaples.*

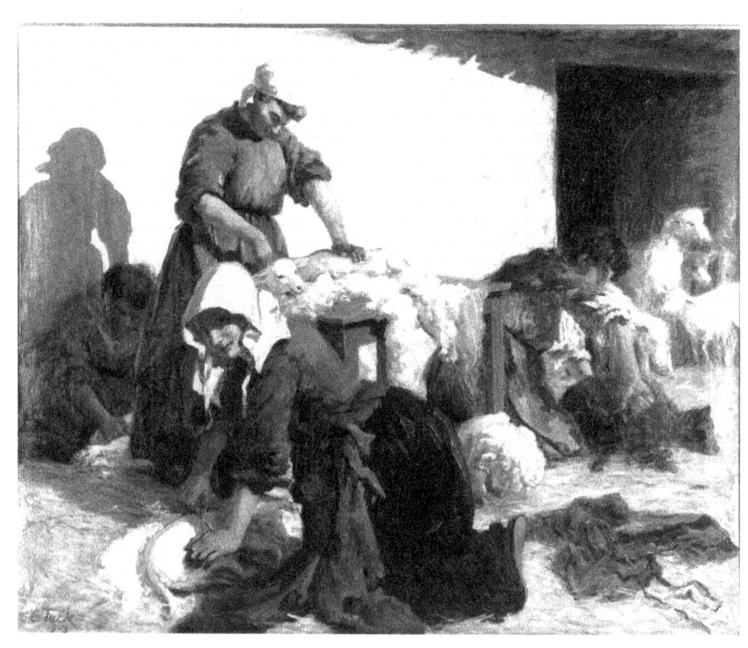

Marie Tuck: *Shearing the Sheep.*

Here is a subject, the essence of Australia. The theme was frequently used between 1880 and 1895 by artists, the most famous being Tom Roberts's *The Golden Fleece.* The concern of the painters was to take daily subjects of Australian life and "realise what was going on around them," a suggestion made to the artists by the American art critic Sidney Dickinson. It was a way to show the rural activities of a huge, new country in rapid expansion. With Jean-Francois Millet, Jules Breton, Jules Bastien-Lepage and Léon Lhermitte,[85] there are numerous examples in France of this "country" trend. The difference being that in France the painters recorded scenes or landscapes of a country- side threatened by industrial growth. One thinks here of *Depart pour les champs (Departure for the Fields)* and *Le Semeur (The Sower)* by Jean-François Millet. In Australia, the developing agriculture was magnified. Less reflective or contemplative, the Australians interested themselves in activity, movement and harsh male labour. But what in Australia was strong, masculine labour, in Picardy became "strong, feminine labour." In Marie Tuck's painting, it is women who shear the sheep - a domestic duty of women while the men were in the fields or at sea. The position of the women, headgear undone, rolled-up sleeves, all translate or indicate effort. Here Marie Tuck "frenchified" an Australian theme. At that time there were large flocks of sheep in the Canche, Authie and Somme Bays, which were moved along the estuaries and of which the American painter and photographer Eanger Irving Couse[86] left many fine photographs.

The fish market theme was used several times by Marie Tuck. Two works entitled *The Fish Market* are in Australia, one at Mt Torrens and the other in Adelaide. Both are set in Etaples. The preparatory work puts into place the tones. The final work done in a Paris studio, uses the same angles, characters and light. From one subject to another, Marie Tuck remained faithful to her actors and the bent old woman on the right in *The Fish Market* is seated on the left in *The Gossips.*

The Gossips chat on a doorstep near the water pump, a favourite place to talk and conspire. Set in a narrow lane inhabited by fishermen and their families, the scene is presented with a "da sotto" perspective which draws the eye from the ground upward, giving the women a pleasing fullness on a large sized canvas. Here nothing has escaped the realistic tradition of the 19th c. and one thinks of Steinlen's common people of Paris, also of Gustave Doré's paintings.

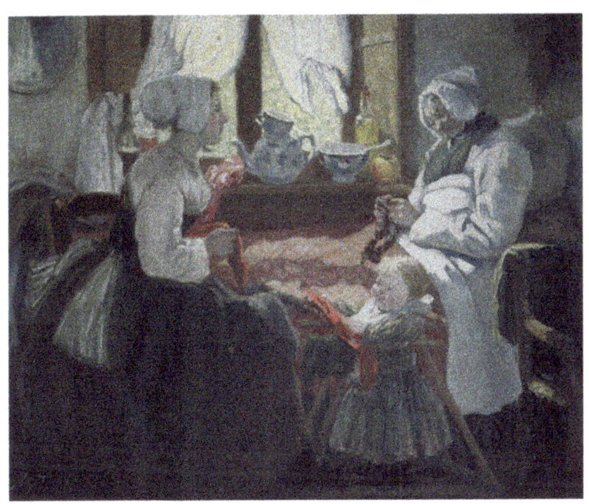

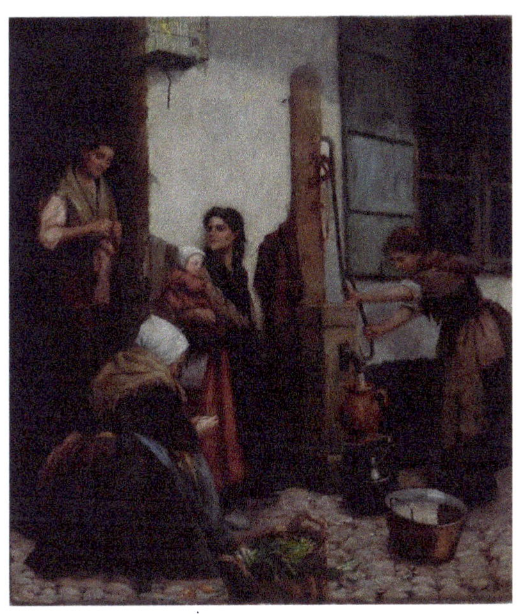

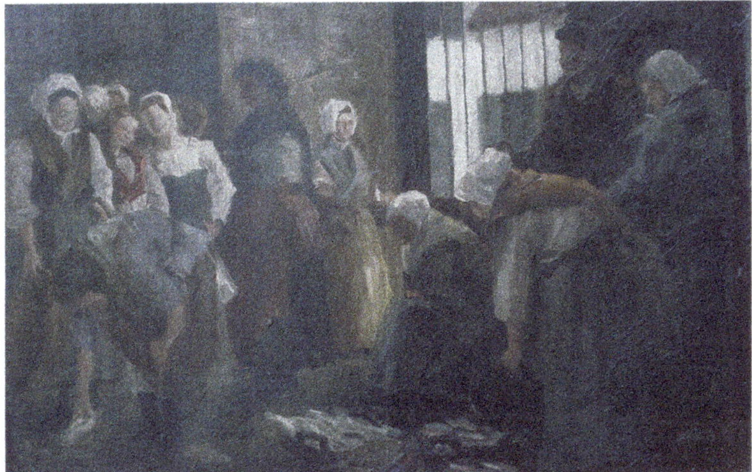

Marie Tuck: *The Gossips* (above).

Marie Tuck: *Confidences* (above left).

Marie Tuck: *The Fish Market* (left).

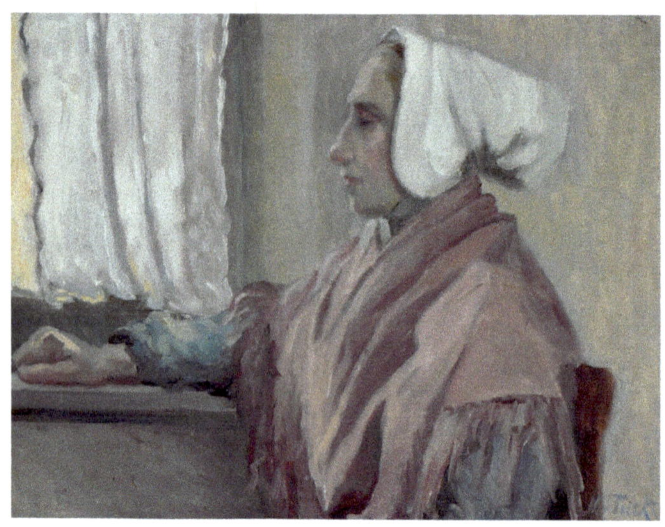

Marie Tuck: *Portrait of a Breton Woman.*

This work represents a close-up of a woman, her arm resting on a window sill. She is wearing a "calipette," the bonnet or headgear worn by the seamen's wives, in current usage until the First World War. The palette of browns, mauve and grey evoke that of Rupert Bunny's *Near Etaples*, painted a few years earlier.

Confidences assembles in an interior, a bed-ridden grandmother with her daughter and small granddaughter who keep her company. The foreground is in semi-darkness (in contrast to the natural light above). It makes one think of a photograph by E. I. Couse where a similar grouping of three generations stand alongside the quay in Etaples.[87] Both painting and photograph are like a reference to the "three ages of life," a theme quite common in that period of out-and-out symbolism.

At the time Marie Tuck was in Etaples, the "Pond" was to be found in today's Place Jeanne d'Arc. It was a rainwater-filled reservoir, a large pond which served as a drinking place for animals as well as a laundry washing place. The lime-washed facades of the old houses with red-tiled roofs lined one side of the pond with St Michel Church[88] in the background - a picturesque place and a fine subject to paint; one which attracted Henri Le Sidaner, Eugene Chigot and Eugène Boudin. Marie Tuck also chose this setting but this time, to paint it at night.

The pond in the foreground covers half the painting, with a reflection of the church spire - caught by the painter 's eye in its fleeting presence. The windows, the house doors and the church nave in the background of the composition are reduced to luminous blobs. Nocturnal painting was frequent at the turn of the century: Jean-Charles Cazin, Henri Duhem, Henri Le Sidaner, Fries Thaulow and H. O. Tanner, all liked and produced villages in the moonlight.

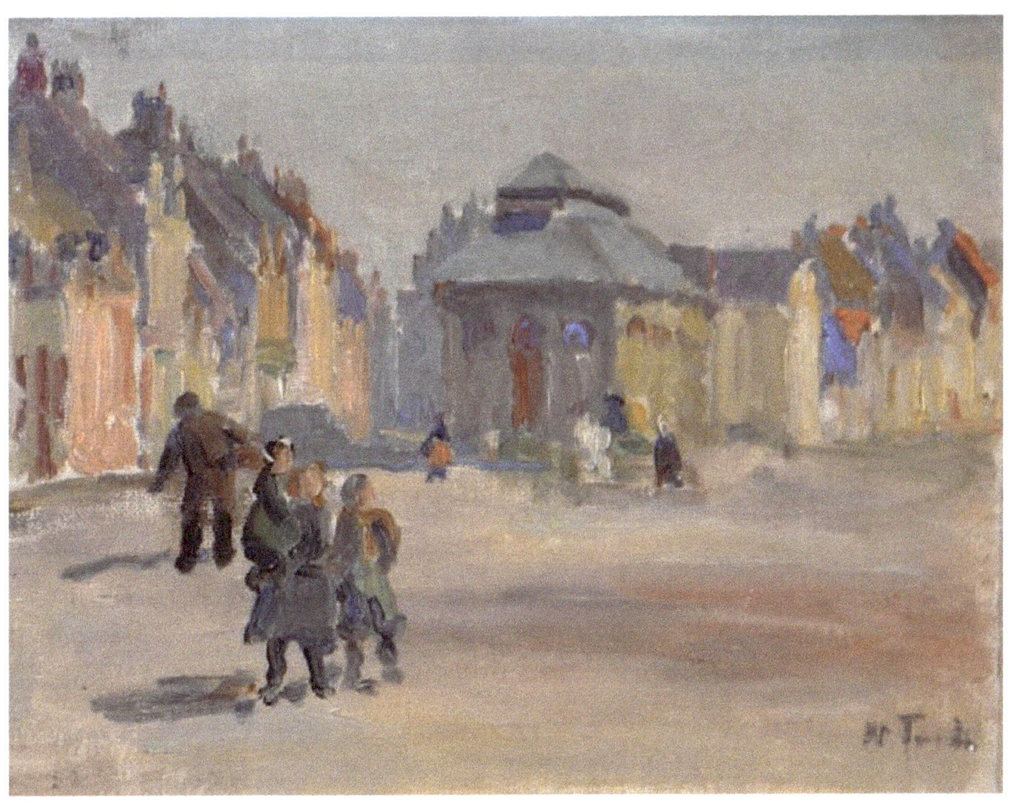

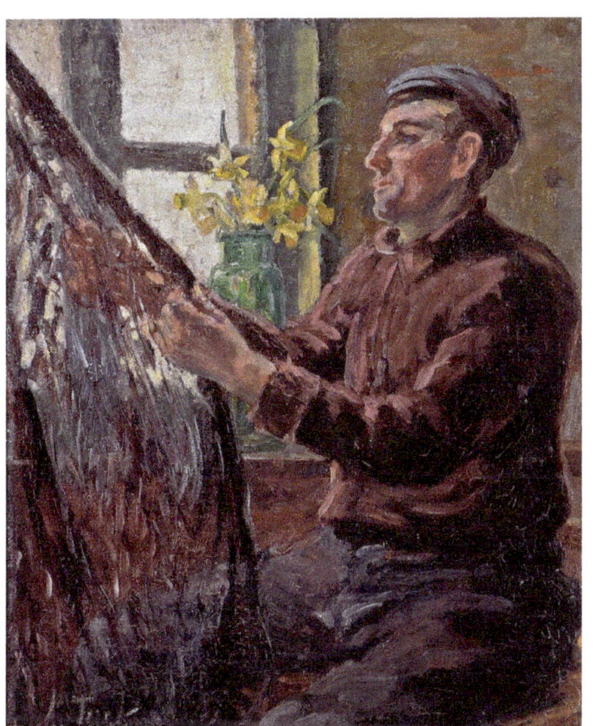

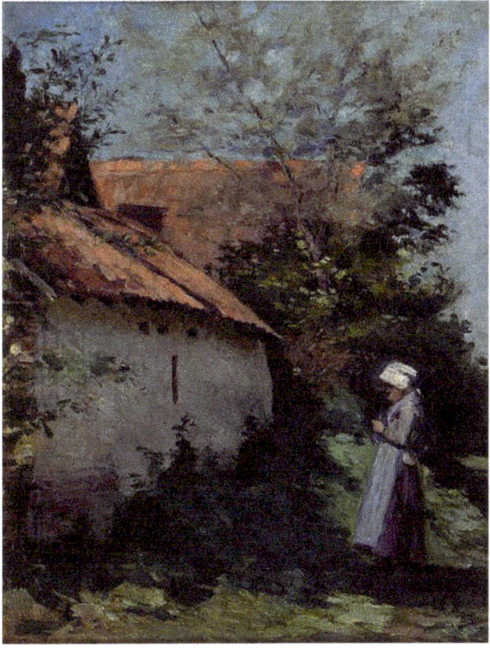

Marie Tuck: *Etaples*, 1947 (above); *Mending the Nets, Brittany* (above left) and *Etaples,* 1907.

AUSTRALASIAN TRAVELLERS

SOME JUST STOPPED ON THEIR WAY...

Among Australasian painters who went to Europe in the conquest of art, some settled on the coast of Picardy and produced work in abundance. Others, in quest of incentives, or simply friendly contacts, did no more than pass.

Alice Muskett

Alice Muskett,[89] a pupil of Julian Ashton[90] in Sydney, opens the long list of travellers. She arrived in Paris in 1895 where she attended the Académie Colarossi. Then, she spent summer in Etaples, returning the following year. In an interview with the Sydney *Daily Telegraph*, she spoke of the artistic life in Etaples: she had paid a visit to lso Rae "who was doing remarkable work and who had a studio there;" to James Quinn, "one of the holders of a Victorian scholarship," as well as to a Mr Hale of New Zealand. She also mentioned the Hotel Ioos "the walls of which are divided into panels and decorated by artists who frequent this little coast town" and amongst which she had remarked on the works of lso Rae and Dudley Hardy.[91]

Alice Muskett favoured still life, genre scenes, and highly symbolic compositions with people. She was also the author of poems and short stories, which she illustrated with a good sense of layout and colour, much in the manner of Eugene Grasset.

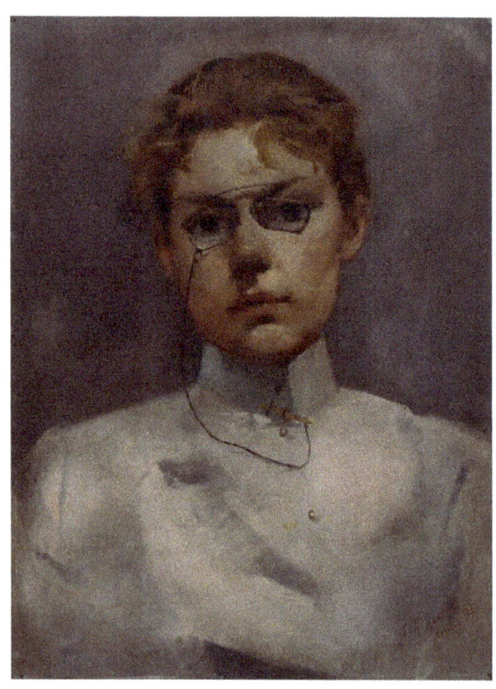

Julian Ashton: *Portrait of Alice Muskett.*

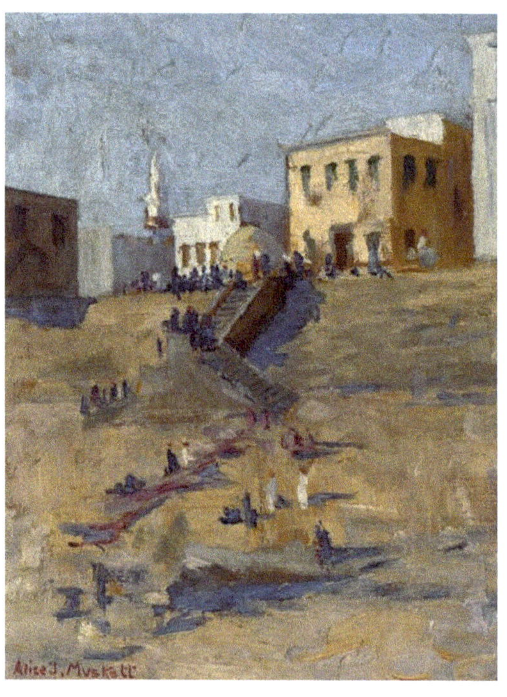

Alice Muskett: *The Landing Place, Esna*. 1911.

Cristina Asquith Baker

Daughter of a Presbyterian minister, Cristina Baker[92] commenced her artistic studies at the National Gallery School, Melbourne. In 1891 she enrolled at the school of art which Tudor St George Tucker and E. Phillips Fox had just opened. A central figure in Fox's large painting, Students in Fine Arts, she became the favourite pupil of the master. From 1902 to 1906, she travelled in Europe, entered the Académie Julian and worked with the American painter Charles Lasar.[93] She shared her Parisian studio with Ada Plante, "living on tea and biscuits," and prepared her admission to the Salon. She was successful in 1904. During the summer she went to Etaples. Her painting, *Spring Roses*, gives a good idea of her style. This still-life is approached with great liberty of execution, treated in a very modern manner. In 1906 Cristina Baker returned to Melbourne where she exhibited landscapes, portraits and still-lifes, and taught drawing and painting.

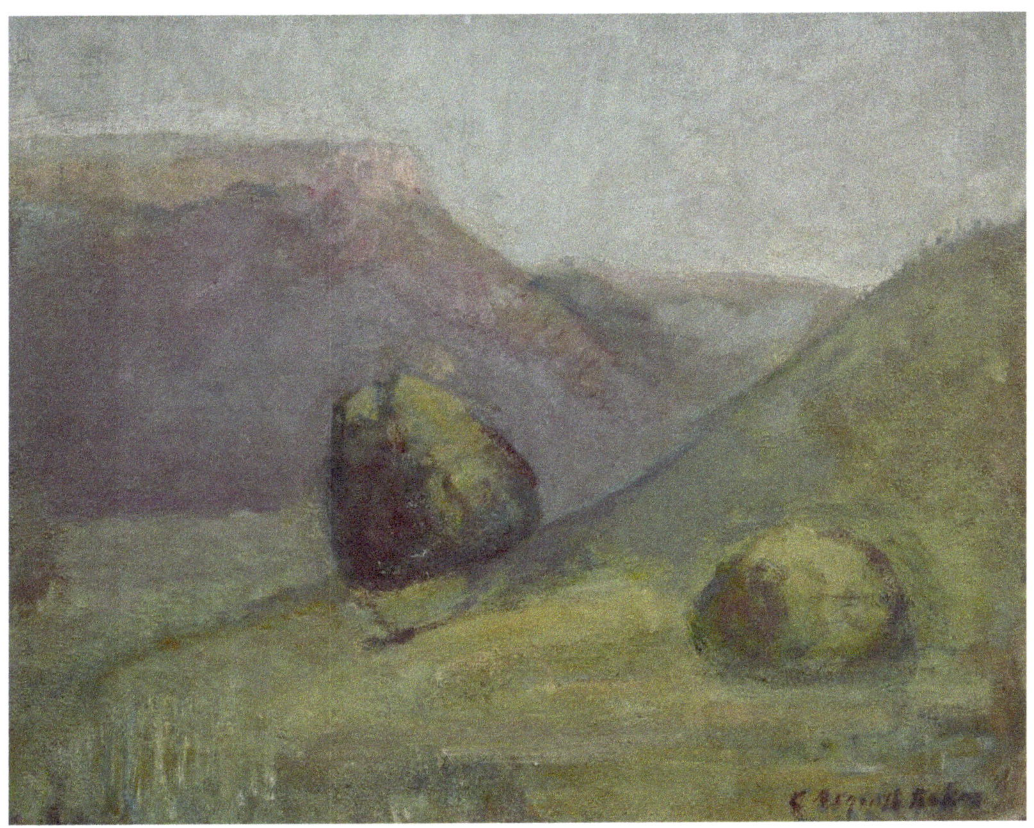

Christina Asquith Baker: *Landscape.*

Constance Jenkins

Constance Jenkins[94] was among the innovative young women painters from classes given by Bernard Hall, 95 National Gallery School, Melbourne. Her work was praised at the 1907 Women's Work Exhibition. She obtained a travelling grant from the State of Victoria and visited the Etaples colony in 1910.

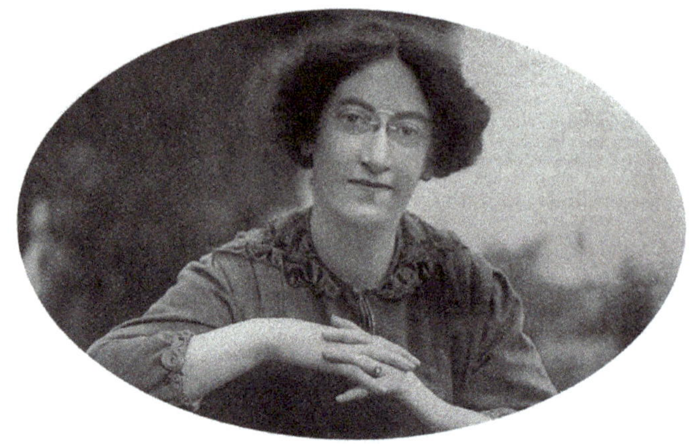

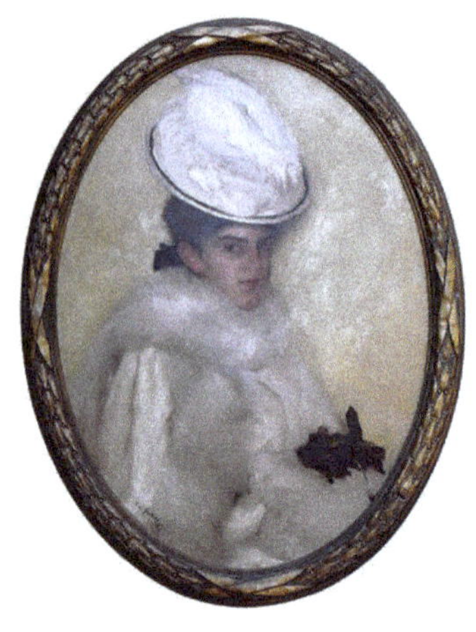

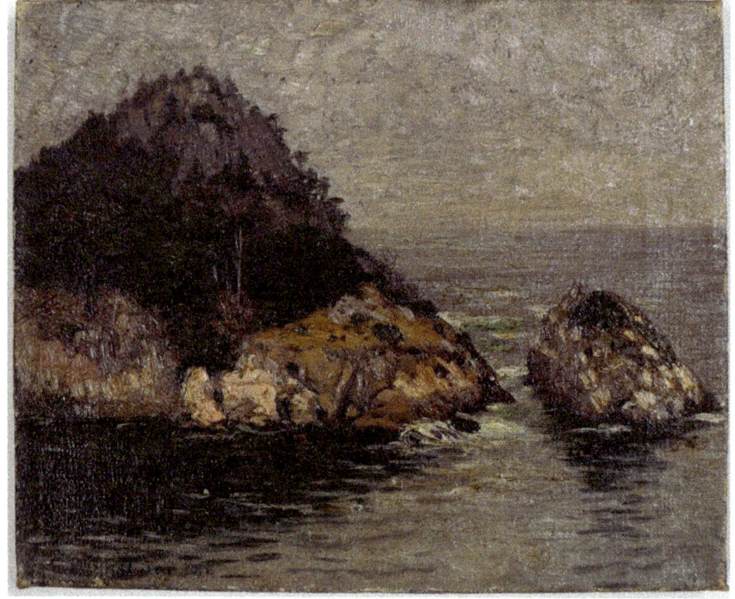

Constance Jenkins, 1910.

Constance Jenkins, *The Woman in White* (1907).

Constance Jenkins: *The Sea*, (1910).

Winifred Honey

Winifred Honey[96] arrived in Melbourne with her family and took courses at the National Gallery School, where she obtained the prize for anatomical drawing. In 1911, she was granted a travelling scholarship and a year later, she was in London, completing her training and starting her career as a painter. Interiors, outdoor nudes, and full-length portraits - in the manner of John Singer Sargent, made up her repertoire. After the First World War, she worked in watercolour and sent *Twilight* to the 1919 Salon: "This study of a scene in Etaples previously exhibited with the Royal Institute, is a successful treatment of light and shade not often attempted in the difficult medium of watercolour."[97]

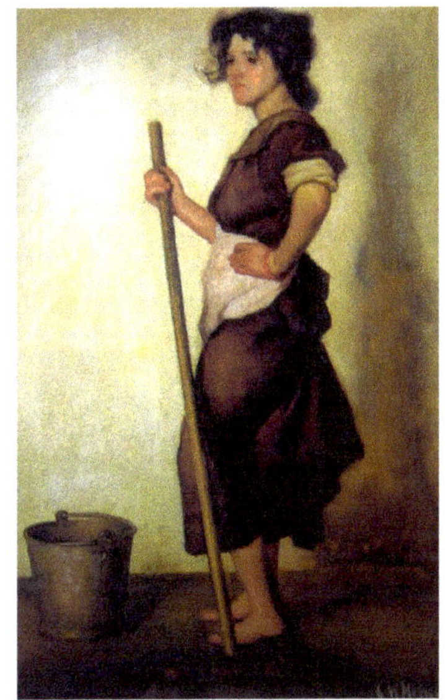

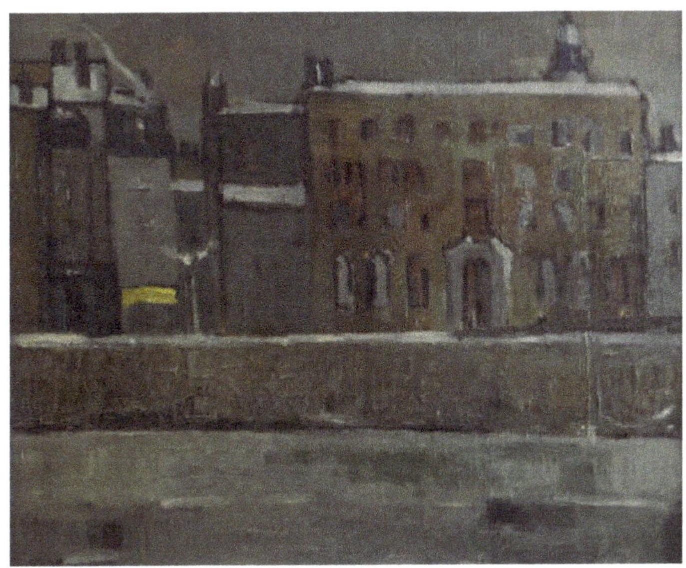

Winifred Honey: *Girl with a Broom* (1907); *Between the Dark and the Daylight, Brittany.*

Bessie Gibson

Bessie Gibson [98] trained at Central Technical College, Brisbane. At 35, she went to France and lived in Paris for a number of years. In 1909 she was in Etaples and Montreuil. She exhibited at the Salon des Artistes Français (1912-1939) and at the Salon d'Automne (1922-1934), portraits in the style of Frances Hodgkins, her professor at the Académie Colarossi. After a career essentially European, she returned to Australia in 1947. Bessie Gibson is one of the artists recently rediscovered through exhibitions.[99]

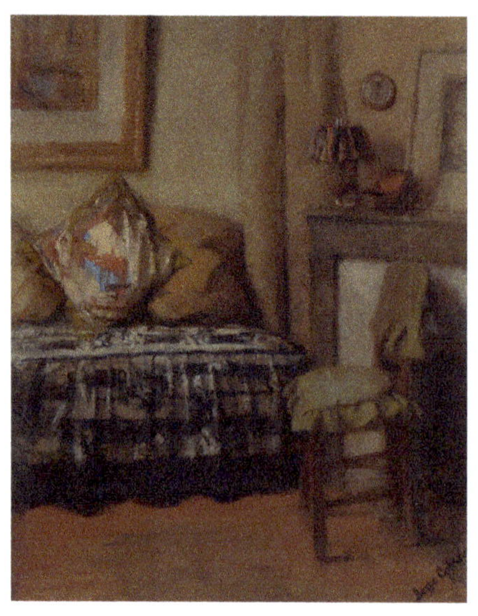

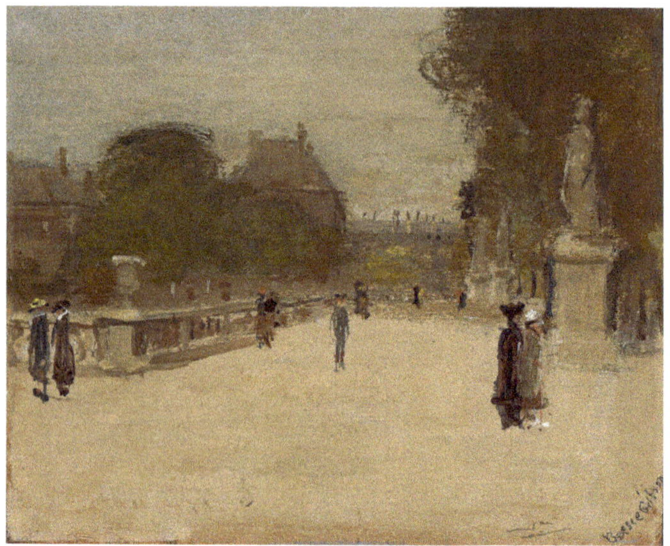

Bessie Gibson: *A Corner of My Studio, Paris*, courtesy Lawsons; *Study for the Luxembourg Gardens.*

Maud Burge

Born in Wellington (New Zealand), Maud Burge[103] was also a friend of Frances Hodgkins. Her Pig Market,[104] painted around 1910, shows great skill in the use of watercolour.

John Barclay Godson

Painter, engraver and printer, John Barclay Godson[105] taught drawing and engraving in Auckland (New Zealand) and then settled in Sydney. Around 1925 he immortalised - through his engravings - some remarkable Montreuil monuments: St Saulve Church, the Court, to which should be added the Etaples Jetty.

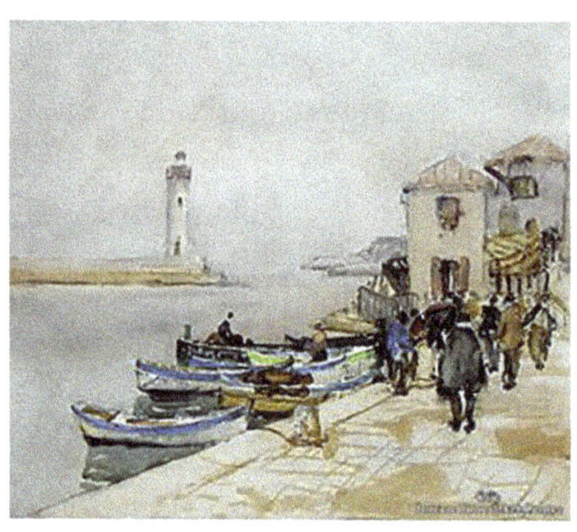

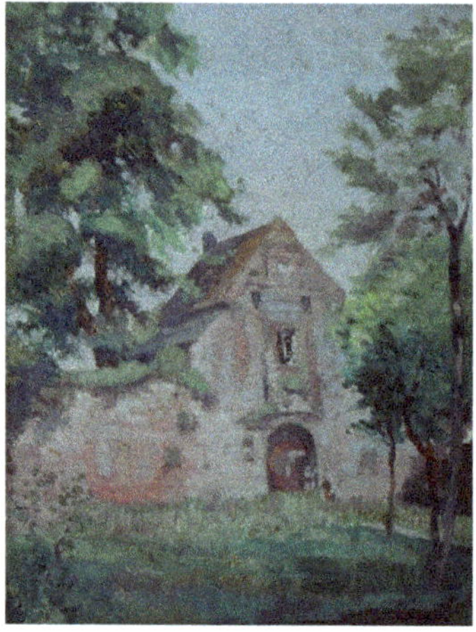

Maude Burge: *Fishing Boats, Brittany* (left)

John Barclay Godson: *Entrance to the Old Walls, Montreuil.*

Frances Hodgkins

Daughter of a New Zealand painter, Frances Hodgkins[100] worked firstly with Girolamo Nerli in Melbourne and reached Europe in 1901. She travelled and painted, and gave art lessons for a living. From May to August 1909, she gave a summer course in Montreuil where she exhibited her students' work. Though we have no trace of her work of this period, her Picardian stay was mentioned in a letter addressed to her mother dealing with the pilgrimage of Saint-Josse - a sight of an incredible demonstration of native superstition seen by a talkative New Zealander: "I must tell you of an amusing jaunt we had on Sunday. We took a train to the little village of St Josse to see a pilgrimage to kiss the sacred relics of the good St Josse and to dip in the holy pool and be cured of all one's devils... [We] followed the crowd and squeezed into the little chapel and up to the altar to kiss the sacred relics, religious fervour ran high, music, gutting candles, incense, the Madonna-like faces of some of the women, devout and rapt all helped to carry one on with a wild sort of surge towards the altar. I was suddenly swept on and found myself almost in front of a priest, a fat, bloated, sensual, pagan beast who only wanted a few vine leaves to turn him into Bacchus - he was holding out to the struggling crowd a large waxen leg and foot - the good St Josse's, which each one kissed and passed on but not till they had dropped a penny into a golden coffer held under their noses by another priest.

I clutched my little Tiki-man, and decided it was good enough for me and wedged out of the crowd followed by an ugly look from the fat Satyr at the altar. It was not a pretty sight at all. What pagans we all are!..."[101]

Frances Hodgkins returned periodically to New Zealand and in 1912, exhibited some watercolours in Melbourne. A painter with a strong personality, eccentric and witty, she formed a friendship with two "avant-garde" English artists, Ben Nicholson and Barbara Hepworth.[102] She also "preferred not to exhibit among artists with whom [she] had nothing in common," yet her name was among those listed at the 1940 Venice Biennale.

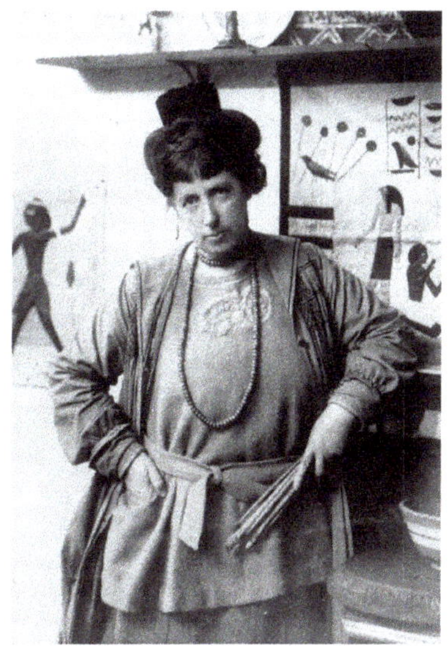

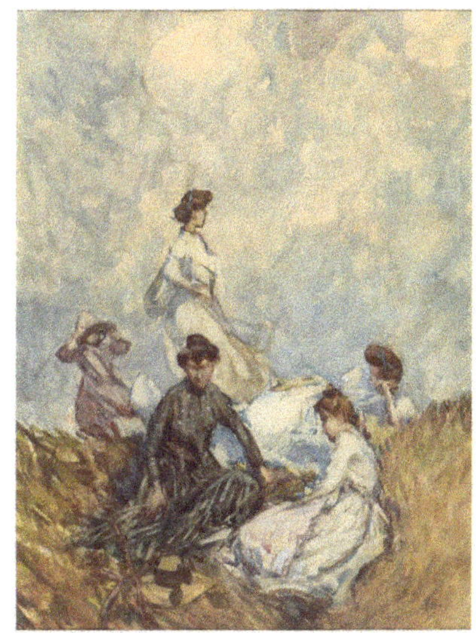

Frances Hodgkins (left)

Frances Hodgkins: *The Hilltop* (1908)

OTHERS LINGERED ...

E. Phillips Fox

E. Phillips Fox[106] was the first Australian painter to spend a summer in Etaples in 1887. He wrote to Tom Roberts: "I am now in the country painting from nature, and think the work I am doing an advance upon former efforts. I have become acquainted with a Mr Harrison here who is considered a very good man. He has been very friendly and it was he who reminded me of you. Speaking to him this evening, he said: 'You have very good men in Victoria.' and then went on about the Colonial Exhibition in London. He said: 'I was surprised at one man's work exhibited there.' As he did not remember the name, I asked him to describe the pictures, and, if I am not greatly mistaken, they were yours. He wanted to know if you were appreciated - 'Surely work like that is not recognised yet out there.'[107]

The American painter, Birge Harrison had a large studio built in the garden of the Pannier boarding house in Etaples, which he occupied a number of years. His brother, Alexander,[108] worked in Paris and gave painting lessons. Talented outdoors painters, supporters of moderate impressionism, the Harrisons would encourage young artists to find their own feet. They were to highly influence E. Phillips Fox's orientation.

The works by E. Phillips Fox which can be localised as having been done in Etaples, show an explosion of light in his canvases where the yellow plays-off the pink and pale grey. His are generally modestly formulated paintings, with a touch of free expression which gives a foreboding of the hedonic approach which was to come. *The Market Place, Etaples* (see below) is bathed in dazzling light in a range of very clear tones. It seems that, much like Robert Reid[109] and Henri Le Sidaner,[110] the Etaples painters of the 1890's applied paint sparingly on their canvases and used a lighter palette.

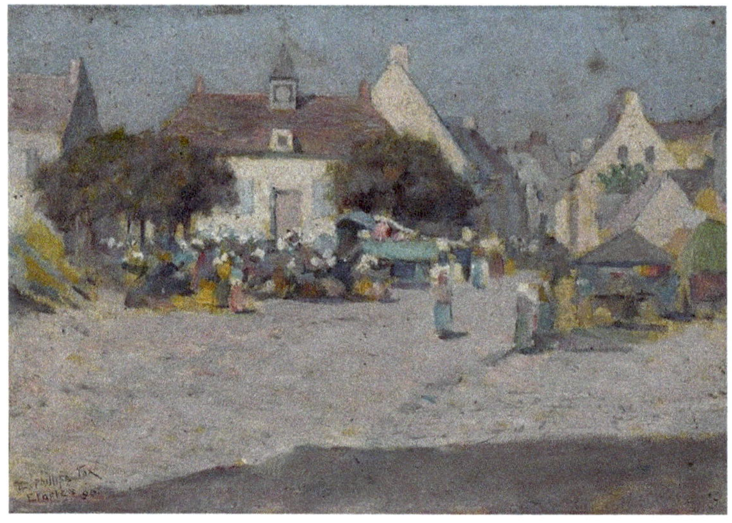

Charles Conder

Following the death of his mother in 1884, Charles Conder[111] was sent from England to Australia. He lived in Sydney until 1888. His uncle, an engineer who took charge of him, did not discourage the young man's artistic talents and Charles Conder commenced as a designer at the *Illustrated Sydney News*. He also began to paint landscapes and to form a friendship with Tom Roberts, who initiated him in the art of outdoor painting in and around Sydney. The purchase of *Departure of S. S. 'Orient'* by the Sydney Museum in 1888, confirmed the notoriety of young Charles Conder. In the same year, he went to Melbourne, joined the Heidelberg School, and designed the catalogue cover for the "'9x5' Impression Exhibition."

In 1890 he returned to Europe and stayed in Paris. He was warmly welcomed by the American painters there: "On arrival I went to see the Julian School, in company of some American artists who showed me round a bit ... [They] tell me that Tucker is the strongest man from Australia in Paris, and Fox is also thought a great deal of."[112] They also informed him on the "stars" of the moment: Bastien-Lepage and Puvis de Chavannes. [113] Louis Anquetin[114] - whom he met at Cormon's, and Henri de Toulouse-Lautrec being among his best friends, Lautrec including him in *Au Moulin Rouge, Aux Ambassadeurs* and *En Cabinetparticulier.*[115] Conder shared the agitated life of Montmartre. With Steinlen, he was a regular customer at the "Chat Noir" or, at the "Mirliton" chez Aristide Bruant, much to the prejudice of Tom Roberts, an unwilling witness of the extravagances of his compatriot. The existence in which Conder "burnt the candle at both ends," shortened his life: he died after a long illness at the early age of forty.

In Paris, Conder decorated Samuel Bing's "Maison del "Art Nouveau" - where Chinese and Japanese art was well represented, exhibited chez Thomas, Boulevard Malesherbes, while his friend Rothenstein painted his portrait in the studio, rue Ravignan. [116]

From 1894, Conder lived mostly in England. He mixed in the elegant London life, frequented the artistic circle of the New English Art Club, retaining only Arthur Streeton among his Australian friends. He spent summer on the French Channel coast, in Dieppe, where he could be found in the company of Walter Sickert, Aubrey Beardsley, Jacques-Emile Blanche[117] and Frits Thaulow, who gave him accommodation. This company speaks volumes with regard to Conder's affinity for decadent Anglo-Saxon painters and the influence they were to have on his painting.

The works by Conder of the Calais region are linked to a stay in Ambleteuse, a seaside resort north of Boulogne-sur-Mer. Florence Humphrey, one of Conder's student in London, invited him to Ambleteuse in summer 1901. While he was there, he met a young widow, Stella Maris McAdam (Mrs Bedford) and fell in love. The marriage took place in Paris, in December of the same year. From this summer visit to French shores in July and August 1901, there remain some works which are fairly representative of Conder: a painted fan, a portrait of *Mrs Bedford*, and a landscape *Ambleteuse Dunes.*

In the above-mentioned work, the painter interprets the seduction of the setting, the summer light which bathes the Channel beach. The space given to the blue sky and to the sea covers two thirds of the canvas. In the rapid strokes done in clear tones, side by side, all is allusive: the beach tents, the silhouettes of the women and children. The slightly plunging view made orderly by the verticals of the tents and the people, with the oblique dune, breathe life into the painting. On the canvas, the artist assembled his first impressions without hesitation nor regret - and the result is successful. It is a rather rare landscape amongst Conder's repertoire.

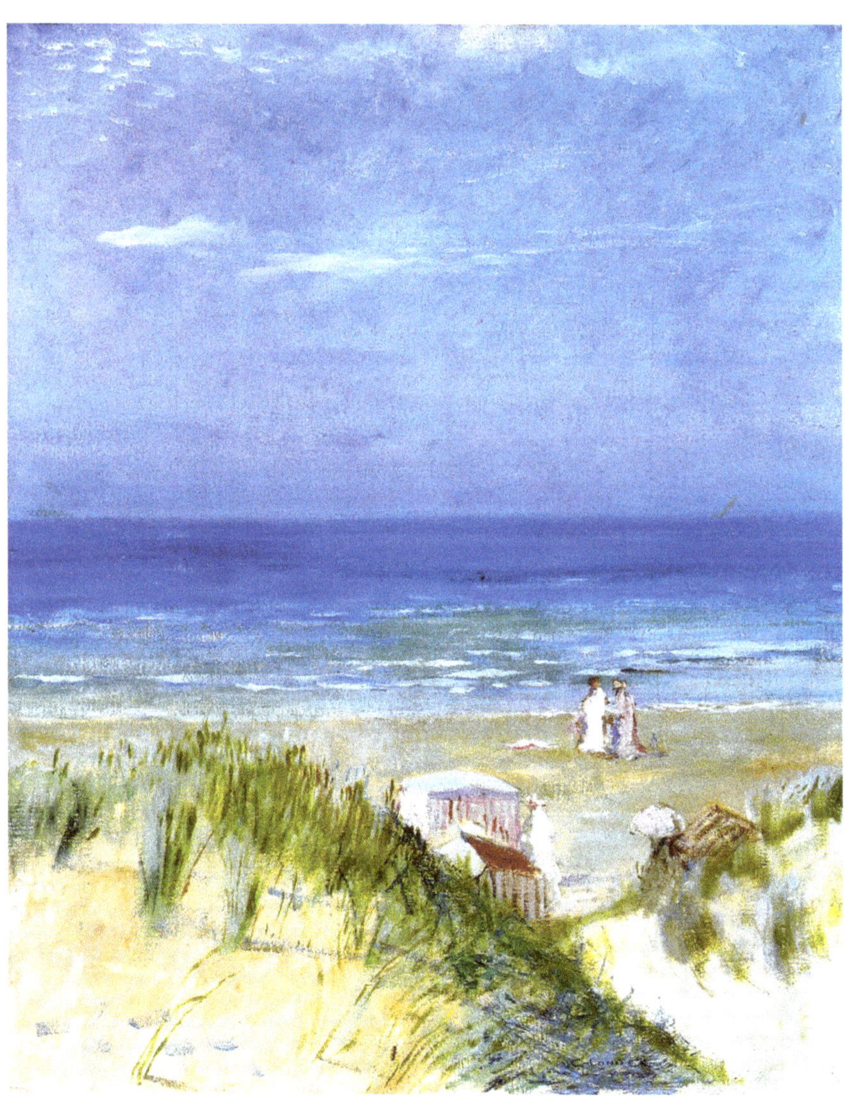

Charles Condor: *Sand dunes*

Grace Joel

Daughter of the owner of the Red Lion Brewery in Dunedin, Grace Joel[118] received a liberal education for a woman, which gave her the chance to show her ability. She studied art in Dunedin and at the Melbourne National Gallery School until 1894. In 1893 she won first prize for a painting of a female nude and rapidly established her individuality at a time when such a theme was always regarded with much circumspection. In Melbourne, she lived amongst the leaders of the Heidelberg School.

She arrived in Europe in 1899 and entered the Académie Julian in Baschet and Schommer's studio. Like many expatriate painters, she divided her artistic activities between Paris and London and exhibited in both capitals: in the Salon des Artistes Français as well as in the Royal Academy. Grace Joel continued to work in the tradition of portrait painting where the group of mother and child was frequent - a subject prized by other women painters like Elizabeth Nourse, Beatrice How or Virginie Demont.[119] Grace Joel was, like Virginie Demont, sensitive to the then growing feminism and women's rights movements.

Between 1903 and 1906, Grace Joel was in Etaples and painted on the theme of the market: a preparatory work for *Market Place* and a final *Etaples Market,* a view of the place d'Etaples done from the rue de Montreuil, with the Town Hall in the background. To these two works should be added, *Etaples Grandfather.* This portrait of an elderly man with its marked light and shade in the style of Rembrandt, shows the artist's father who actually never came to Picardy. The painter perhaps noted "Etaples" due to the popularity of the area: at the time she painted this portrait she lived in London where she died a few years later.

The absence of correspondence,[120] and the discretion of the artist - from a well to do family, explain somewhat why her work remains unknown.

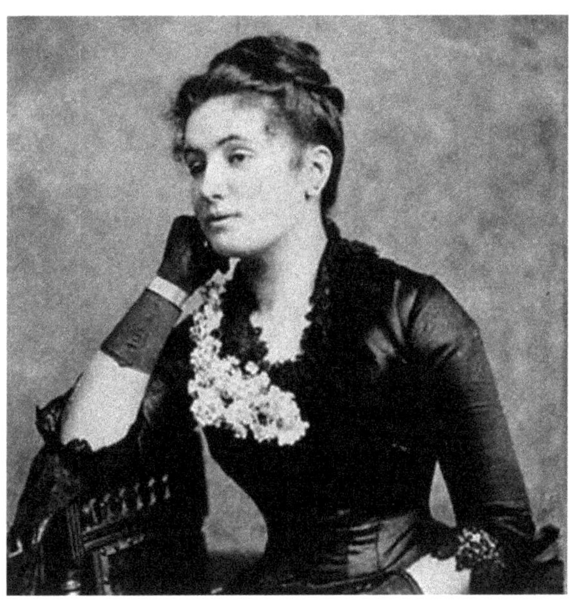

Edward Cairns Officer

When a young student, Edward Cairns Officer[121] met Frederick McCubbin and decided he would become a painter. In 1893 and 1894, he studied at the National Gallery School, Melbourne, and became a pupil of E. Phillips Fox. In 1895, he left Melbourne for Paris and entered the Académie Julian. In the summer, he stayed in Etaples where he met Alison and Isobel Rae, and James Quinn. He quickly became one of the group of the "Picardy painters" and in 1896, with the American Max Bohm, organised the first painting exhibition at Paris-Plage, in the Grand Hotel Casino. The success of this endeavour was hailed by the Australian press: "This year, Mr Officer and Mr Max Bohm organised an exhibition to which all the students and many French and American artists sent contributions. It was held at Paris-Plage, a fashionable watering place in the neighbourhood, and was a great success being attended by well-known society people present in the town and visitors, French, English and American. Mr Officer received the congratulations of the press on the success of the undertaking, and also for the excellence of his contributions. The *New York Herald* wrote as follows: 'Mr Max Bohm of Cleveland, USA, and Mr E. C. Officer, of Melbourne, Australia, are to be warmly congratulated upon the success of an undertaking not easy of accomplishment ... Among the exhibitors were Miss lso Rae of Melbourne and Mr Quinn ...', and the *journal d'Etaples* added: 'We owe hearty congratulations to Messrs Max Bohm and E. C. Officer. The landscapes by the latter are much admired and one finds in them a freshness and real feeling of nature. The fine *Etaples Landscape,* clearly conveys a blowing wind.'"[122]

Officer returned to Australia in 1900 and settled in NSW on the Darling River. In 1912 he participated in the founding of the Australian Art Association, of which he was president until his death. Above all a landscape artist, a man of the bush and an untiring traveller, he knew how to give his paintings a strength and a realness that attracted attention.

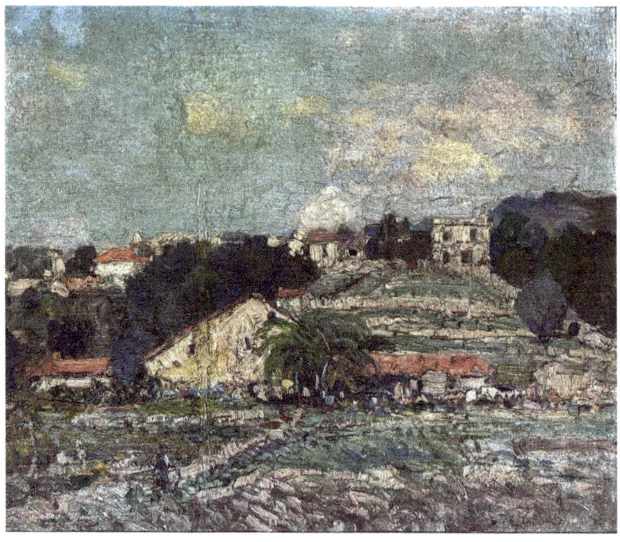

Edward Cairns Officer: *Market Gardens, Southern France.*

James Quinn

James Quinn[123] studied drawing and painting at the National Gallery School, Melbourne, between 1886 and 1893. He obtained a travel grant and set off for Europe. Paris was a great shock to him. Confronted there with what was best, he put his training into question and finally went humbly to Etaples to try to face reality.

From 1896 to 1900, Quinn was in Etaples during the summers. He lodged chez Ioos and frequented E. C. Officer and the Rae sisters. *People Resting Under a Tree, Girl Carrying a Basket of Fish, Fishing Boat, Etaples Fishing Family, Nativity, Mother and Child,* are among the works produced during his Picardian stays. In 1898, Eugene Chigot noted: "a sound study of a child and a poor woman with a well observed usage of blacks." Still in Etaples in 1900, he exhibited at the Artistes Français.

His departure for London in 1902 corresponds with the time of his marriage to Blanche Guernier. He became the portraitist in vogue and honoured commissions from Chamberlain and the Duchess of York. He also became a member of the London Portrait Society and the Royal Society of Portrait Painters, as well as exhibiting in London and Paris.

Quinn returned to Australia in 1935. Sociable and a lover of good food, he lived in an environment of journalists and writers. Though a traditional painter, his friendships were diverse and he participated in the artistic life of Melbourne, notably in the Victorian Artists' Society.

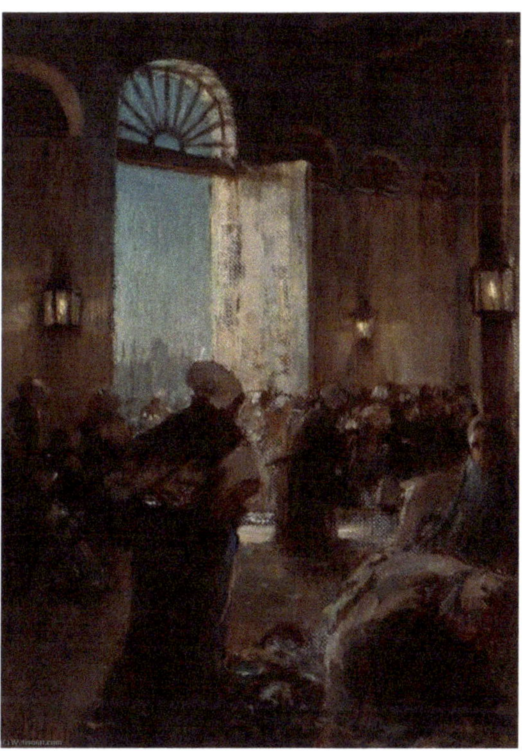

James Quinn: *Fish Market at Etaples, France.*

Eleanor Ritchie Harrison

Eleanor Ritchie[124] attended the National Gallery School, Melbourne, with Eugene Von Guérard and decided she would become a painter. She further continued her studies in London and Paris. While working outdoors, or on the spot, in the countryside around Paris, she met her future husband, Birge Harrison. However, Birge, of fragile health, contracted malaria and to recuperate, he and his wife left for America. They lived the life of adventurous pioneers among Indian tribes of New Mexico and after moving to the East Coast, returned to Europe. Eleanor resumed her studies with Benjamin-Constant, Jules Lefèbvre and Francois Nicolas Feyen-Perrin, a seascape painter. In the summer of 1886, the couple were to be found in Etaples, chez Mme Pannier. After a trip to Melbourne in 1889, they returned to America where Eleanor died in 1895.

Scattered over the world, for the most part in private collections, her work can now hardly be traced.[125] The fame of Birge Harrison long over- shadowed that of his wife but, fortunately, some critics mentioned the quality of the artist: "Her pictures attract attention alike by their technique and by the evidence they present of the artist's capabilities of expressing character. This is notably the case with her *Head* which is that of an apple- cheeked old 'paysanne' - instilled with life and feeling; while the female *Peasant in the Woods*, half shy, half sullen, is also a very real person. *A Fisherwoman* introduces us to a picturesquely treated interior with the figure of the 'poissarde' seated with her back to the window from which a strong light streams into the room, the difficulty of the subject being skilfully surmounted."[126]

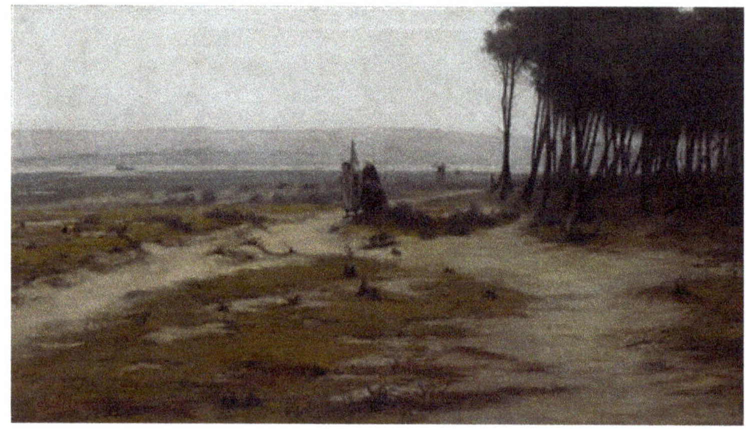

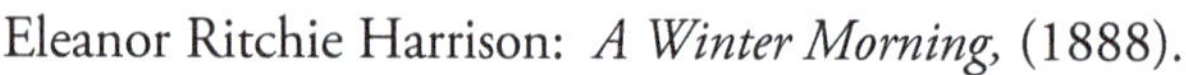

Eleanor Ritchie Harrison: *A Winter Morning,* (1888).

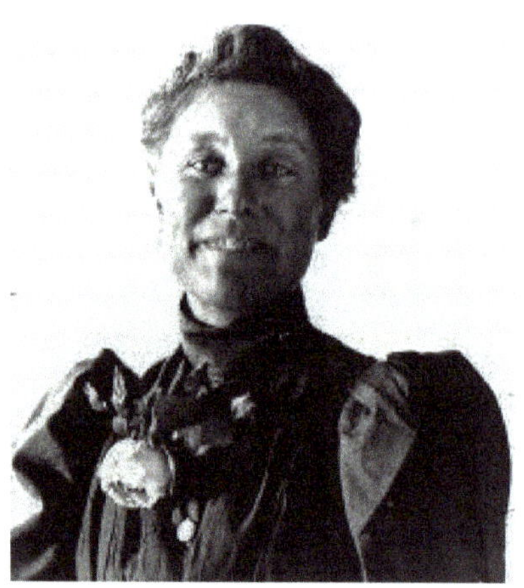

Eleanor Ritchie Harrison.

John Peter Russell

John Peter Russell[127] was considered as a character among the expatriate painters. He came from a wealthy family whose fortune was made in the railway and naval construction industries.

While his father, who wanted John Peter to take over the family business, became irritated at seeing his son losing his time drawing, his mother encouraged the young man's vocation. The death of his father in 1879 and the fortune he inherited allowed John Peter Russell to launch into an artistic career. He left for London two years later, travelling to Europe with Tom Roberts, with whom he began a friendship. In London, he entered the Slade School with Alphonse Legros.[128] The academic nudes which Russell produced around 1886 have many affinities with those of Legros and Jean-Charles Cazin:[129] the same angular features and use of material such as chalk and sanguine.[130] When Legros confided that there was nothing more he could teach him, Russell went to Paris. Chez Cormon, he met Louis Anquetin, Emile Bernard,[131] Armand Guillaumin,[132] Toulouse-Lautrec, Gauguin and, above all, Van Gogh of whom he painted a fine subtle portrait. With Vincent, he shared enormous admiration for Japanese prints. He knew Etaples well which he evokes in letters to Tom Roberts,[133] but it does not seem that he worked there.

In spring of 1887, he was a little further south at Longpré-les-Corps-Saints, between Abbeville and Amiens, where he stayed in the company of Marianna.[134] It was there he painted *Peonies & Head of a Woman, Portrait of Marianna, Wife of the Artist in the Garden at Longpre*, and *Bouquet of White Peonies.* The works produced in Picardy borrow the Japanism of the time in their liberty of setting and the palette of whites, pinks and blues.

Russell, who loved the sea and possessed a yacht, discovered Belle-Ile in 1886. It was there he met Claude Monet[135] - the prince of impressionists - whom he much admired and whose influence was decisive for his painting. Many at that period fled the agitation of Paris: Paul Gauguin stayed in Brittany and Vincent Van Gogh, in the Midi, whereas Russell became passionate over Belle-Ile and, shortly after his marriage to Marianna, had a large house built in a wild corner of the island. In his "English Castle," he would receive travelling artists, including Rodin for whom Marianna served as a model. On Belle-He, Russell painted impressionist canvases in flamboyant colours such as The Red Sail - Port of Goulphar. The audacity of the composition as well as the palette and the manner of working, place these paintings among the forerunners of Fauvism.

The death of Marianna in 1908 plunged Russell into profound confusion: he burnt a number of paintings, sold his house, and, eventually remarried. During the First World War, he worked at London Hospital and then, returned to Sydney where he spent his time either yachting in the harbour or taking care of his garden -"worthy of Monet in its splendour," according to a cousin of his, Thea Proctor, who was also an artist. Russell, who intended to donate his collection of impressionist works to the City of Sydney, had to abandon the project due to the indifference of the responsible representatives.

Having had the single chance to meet Monet on Belle-Ile, John Peter Russell has for too long been classed among the impressionists. The fact is that, in Brittany and in the Midi, he produced canvases which go beyond aesthetic impressionism. While Monet in his *Nymphéas* (*Water Lilies*) carries the form towards abstraction, Russell, carries colour to its paroxysm and announces - like a Valtat or a Van Dongen, the imminence of Fauvism. It would be high time to do him justice.

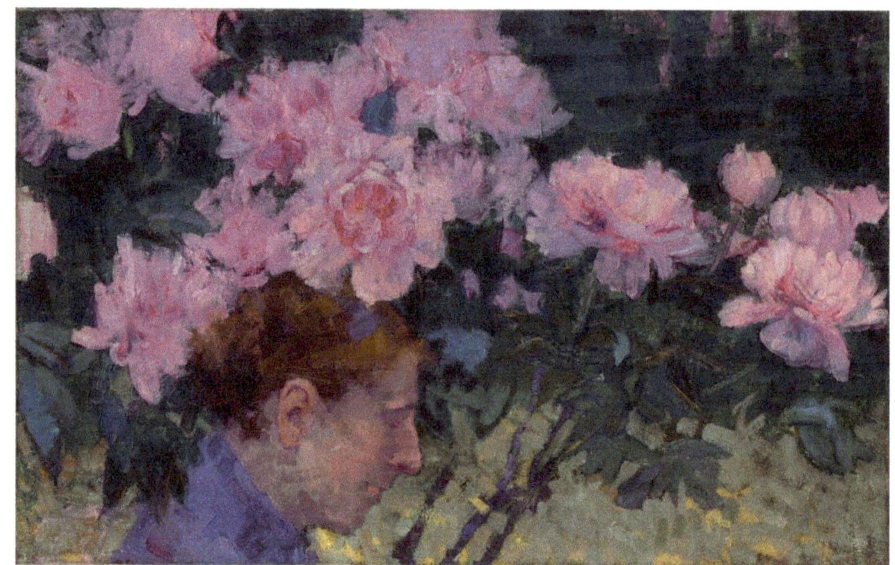

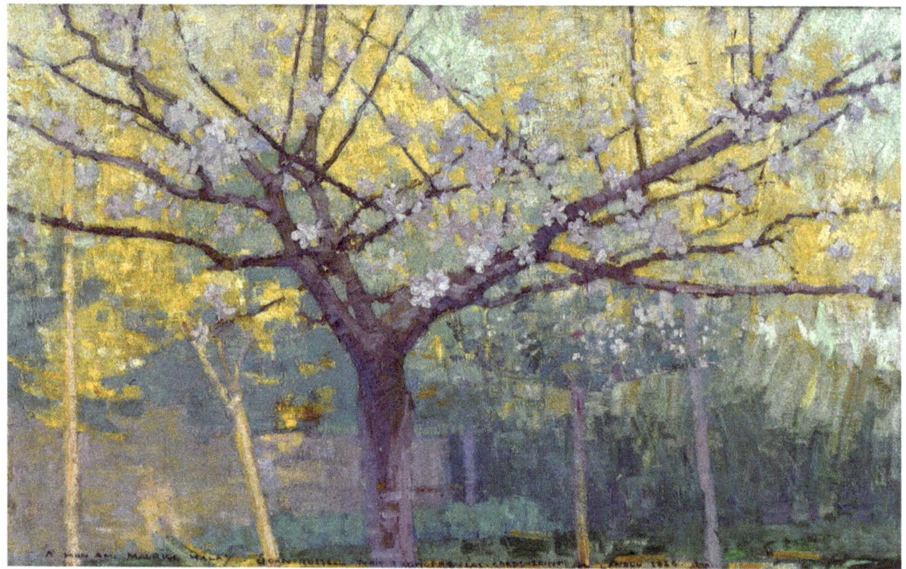

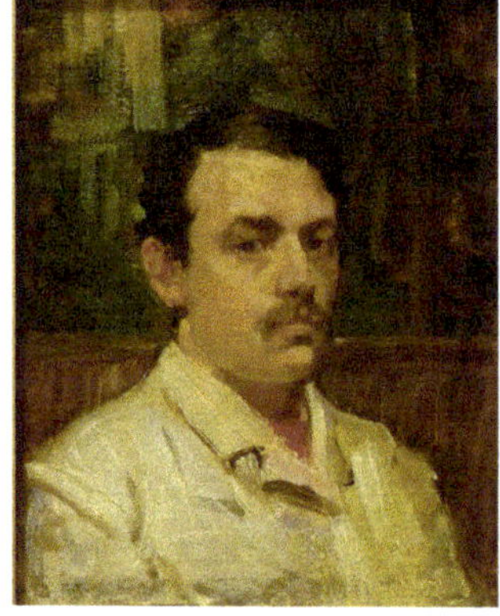

John Peter Russell:
Self-Portrait, ca. 1886

Peonies and head of a Woman (1887) top, National Gallery of Victoria.

The Garden - Longpré-les-Corps-Saints.

Tudor St George Tucker

"Mr Tucker is in the north - at Etaples - where he worked hard all summer. He is likely to try for the Salon this year with an effective picture of an old aged shrimper struggling homeward along the beach, through the purple gloaming of a September evening, with her heavily loaded basket upon her bent old back. Mr Tucker had also another picture worthy of mention - a red-haired fishergirl in the sunlight - besides many interesting studies upon the walls of his cosy little country studio."

Alison Rae[136]

Son of an Indian Army cavalry officer, Tudor St George Tucker[137] went to Australia in 1881 for health reasons. He received a thorough education and became interested in fine arts and music. He attended the National Gallery School in Melbourne where he obtained the drawing prize and exhibited at the Victorian Academy of Arts. In May 1887, he went to Europe in the company of E. Phillips Fox and enrolled at the Académie Julian, passing the Ecole des Beaux-Arts contest brilliantly. From his masters - Robert-Fleury, Gérôme and Bouguereau, he learned technical skill, but his taste led him towards Impressionism. In 1891 and 1892, he was admitted to the Salon de Paris and became known for two works from Etaples: *An Urgent Call* and *Shrimper, Picardy.* "It represents an old fisherwoman returning from shrimping in the early dusk of evening - commented *Table Talk* on 26 August 1892. The view is on the tidal river near Etaples. The grey silt stretches out as far as the eye can reach, the wane light reflected in the pools of water by the receding tide makes the scene look even more dreary. In the background, the thick, banked cloud of the evening mist looks like a shroud ready to be folded down on the lifeless vista, creeping up over the masts of the distant shipping and obscuring the glare of the lighthouse on the far away pier. It is mournful rather than a dreary impression that is created and the eye becomes fascinated by the bent figure of the old woman who, though her back is bent under the weight of shrimping net and bag, tramps sturdily along the edge of firm sand left by the tide. Her face is hard and weather- worn, but in every rugged line, there is character and despite her uncouth attire there is in her bearing and features, the dignity and pathos of toil incessant but never hopeless."

Tudor St George Tucker then returned to Melbourne and in order to make a living, opened an art school with his friend, E. Phillips Fox. Around 1899 he again went to England and took part in the artistic life of London until his death in 1906.

For a long time, Tucker remained in the shadow of the better-known Australian artists. His portraits, nudes, and landscapes show his knowledge of French art with Claude Monet being the painter with whom he had the most affinity.

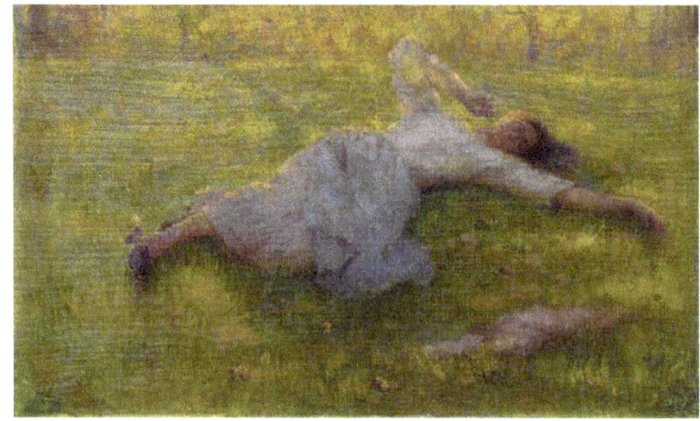

Tudor St George Tucker:
Springtime
To reverse
Etaples/Nov/1890

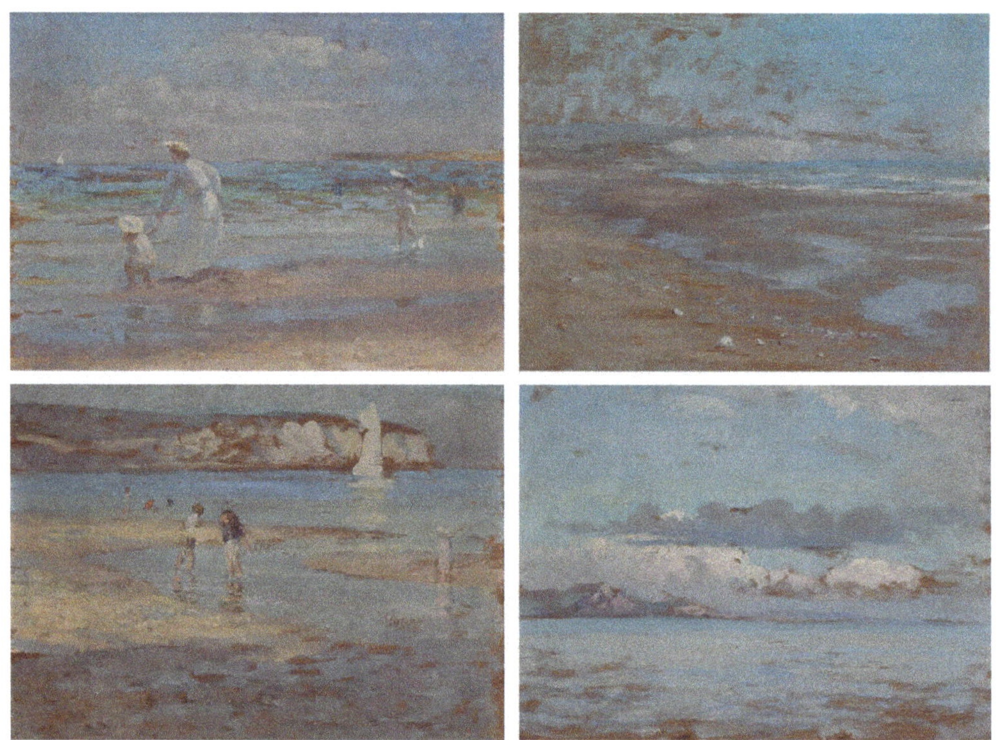

Tudor St George Tucker: *Remembrance of Summer* (1890s).
Courtesy Menzies Art Brands.

AUSTRALIAN PAINTERS AND THE GREAT WAR

The entry of Australia and New Zealand alongside the English in the First World War mobilised Australasian troops - the Anzacs,[138] who paid heavily for their participation in combat on the Western Front in Artois and Picardy. With the concern of keeping a record of this engagement - from 1916 to 1920 - the Australian Government recruited artists who were commissioned for this work. One can hardly imagine the working conditions of these painters, engaged for a period of three to six months, sharing with the rank and file the battles and the life behind the Front. At the end of the conflict, seventeen artists were still working and the title, "Official War Artist", gave the chosen painter recognition.

Given the grade of lieutenant, they used their talent in their own individual way: John Longstaff brushed portraits of military chiefs; Arthur Streeton painted landscapes, places of combat and manoeuvres; Charles Bryant, landing operations in the port of Boulogne; Will Dyson caught, with a few crayon strokes, the battle of Lagnicourt, while Henry Fullwood evoked Picardy in watercolour. As the Australian Commission also solicited from these artists a large work which would immortalize the nation's participation, some paintings such as Amiens, the Key to the West by Arthur Streeton, were realised afterwards.

One associates these artists with those specialised in camouflage - also called at times, "musketeers of brush and pen," who could transform an infantryman into perfect vegetation, or ships into green hills.

Other non-official painters left witness of these difficult times. lso Rae captured on the spot, with means of pastels, the bustling British Camp in Etaples, and even an echo of the September 1917 riots. As for Hilda Rix, the war and its misery became allegories in works like *A Mother of France.*

Charles Bryant, Will Dyson, Fred Leist, Iso Rae, Arthur Streeton, are among those who worked in the proximity of Etaples. The Australian War Memorial, Canberra, and the Imperial War Museum, London, conserve most of their work. In participating in the conflict, Australia forged her identity and William Hughes, Australian Prime Minister at the time, sat at the table among the allies at the 1919 Versailles Treaty.

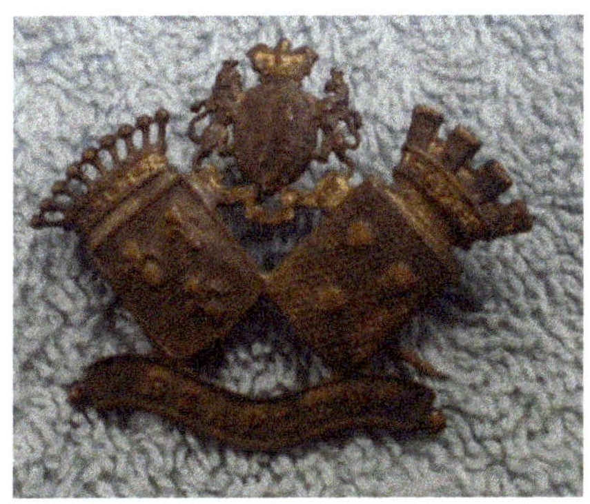

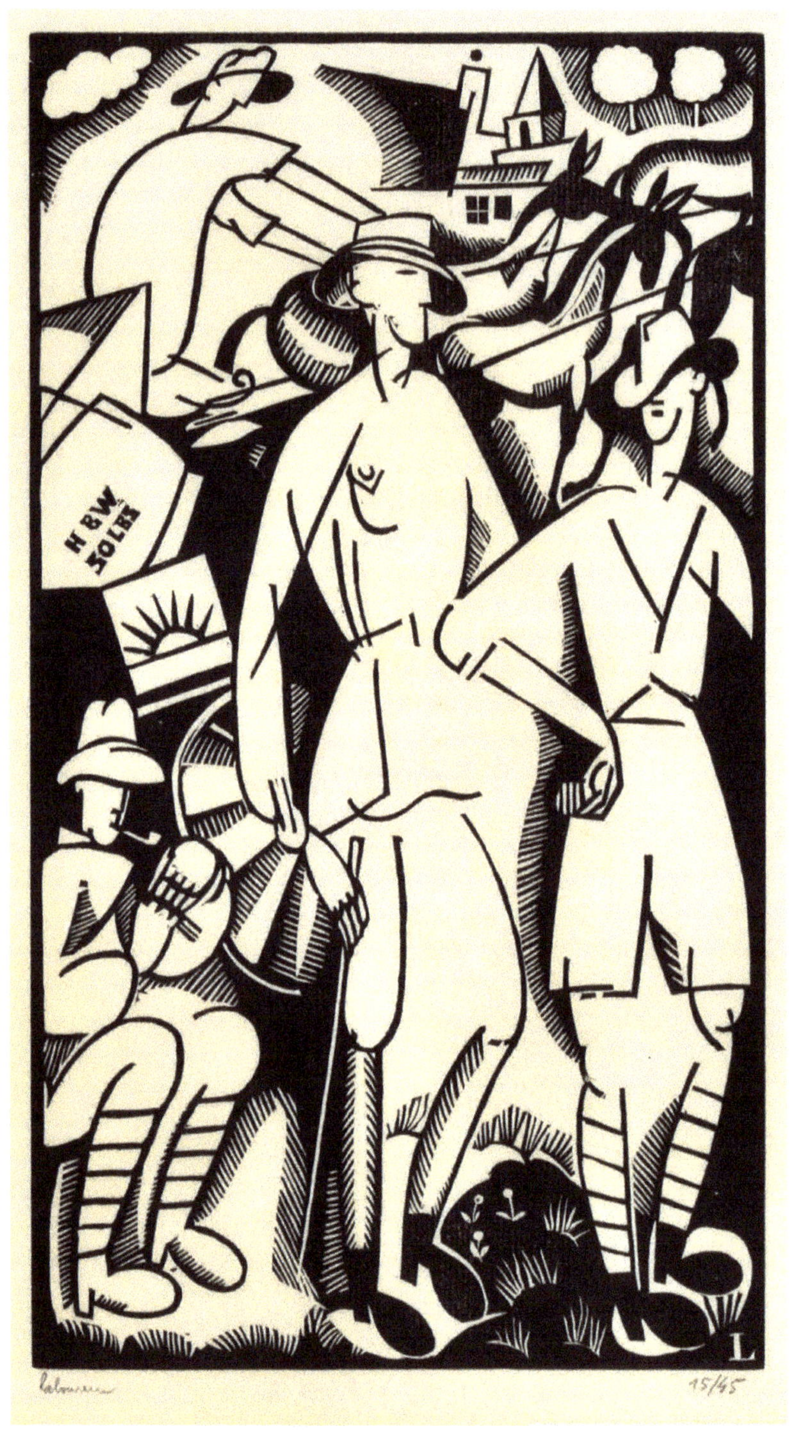

J. E. Laboureur : *ANZACS,* 1918.

Charles Bryant

In Sydney, Charles Bryant[139] learnt drawing with Lister Lister. At 17, he exhibited at the Art Society of New South Wales. In 1908, Bryant joined the painters' colony at St Ives in Cornwall where, in company of Julius Ollson, he painted activities linked to the sea. He became quite naturally a seascape painter and went frequently to Brittany. His canvases belong in the impressionist current and in their finality are close to Will Ashton's work.[140] In London, Bryant was a member of a group of expatriate Australians, a member of the Royal Institute of Oil Painters and the London Sketch Club.

During the First World War, Bryant was an official navy painter in the 2nd A.I.F. Division on the Western Front. He was sent to Boulogne-sur- Mer where he painted the military activities of the port: troop landings, loading and camouflage operations. Nothing dramatic in the work of a painter who captured the agitation of a wartime port. He stayed in the region from December 1917, for one year. In 1922, Bryant returned to Sydney where he pursued his career of official painter in other areas of conflict - notably in New Guinea.

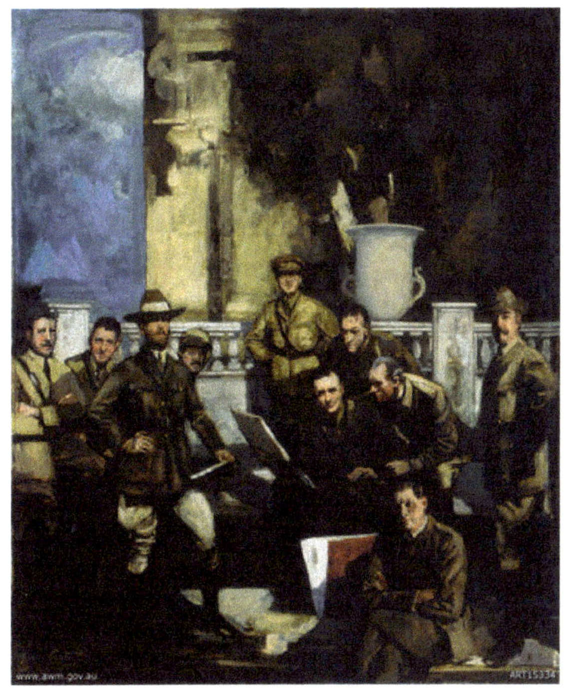

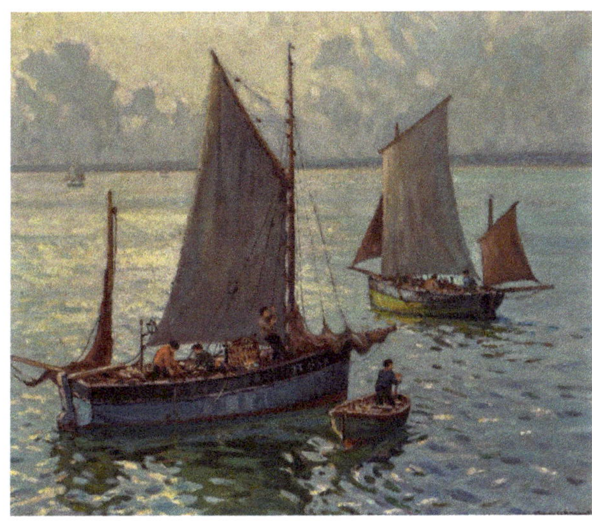

Charles Bryant: *French Fishing Boats.*

George Coates: *Australian War Artists;* standing l-r: (Sir) John Longstaff, Charles Bryant, George Lambert, A. Henry Fullwood, James Quinn, Septimus Power, Arthur Streeton, seated back l-r: Will Dyson, Fred Leist, front: George Bell.

Will Dyson

When studying with George Coates in Melbourne, among Will Dyson's[141] fellow students were George Bell, and Norman and Percy Lindsay - young men who were to become well known figures in Australian art. Dyson discovered the work of the satirical artist, Tom Durkin, and developed his cartoonist talents when he joined the *Daily Herald* in London in 1909. His virulent drawings criticised the politics and the morals and manners of the day, quickly making him a celebrity. He became a friend of H. G. Wells and G.B. Shaw. During the war, he volunteered as a war artist and he was recruited into the A.I.F. in December 1916. He shared the life of the Front, did not hesitate to take risks, and was injured twice in Belguim at Messines and Zonnebeke.

Dyson did not record the grand events of the war, nor did he picture self-assured generals. He was at home among the rank and file and depicted their reactions in exceptional circumstances from which he drew the derision of certain situations with an acute sense of humour. His sketches, therefore, show an inimitable accent. His works are not always localised with precision. When he notes - Mametz, Hazebrouck, Armentieres, Albert or Lagnicourt, these places correspond to the North of France, Artois and Aisne. But the strength of his lines, the sharpness of his eye and the ever-present humour, over-shadow the geographical imprecision. His records cover all Fronts - East and West, as in *The Amateur. Who is cutting hair? You or me?*

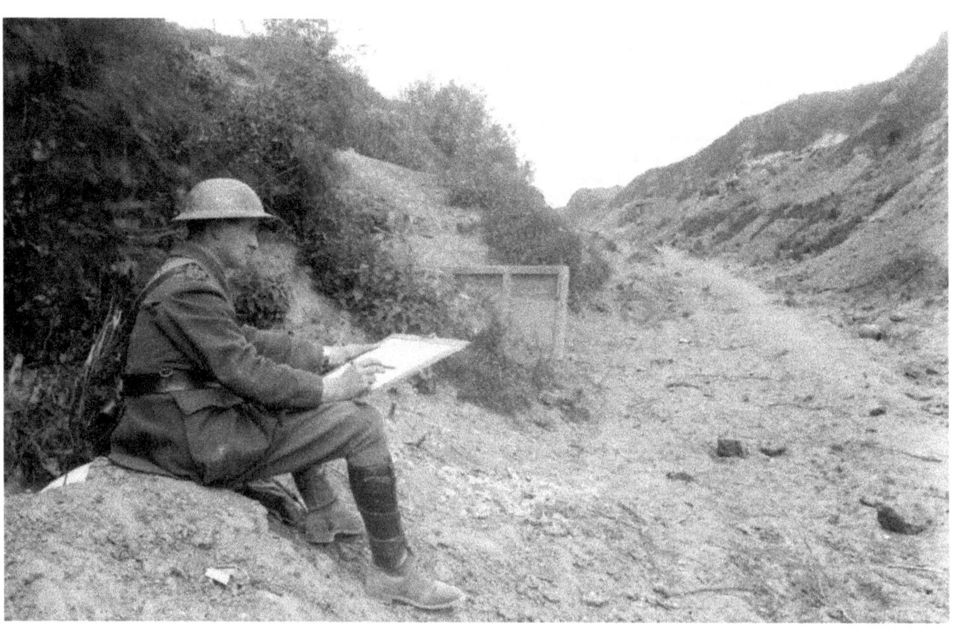

Will Dyson in France 1917.

Henry Fullwood

Born in England, Henry Fullwood[142] arrived in Sydney at eighteen and collaborated as draughtsman with the *Town & Country Journal* and the *Bulletin*. He travelled for his work and therefore acquired a good knowledge of the Australian continent. At Sirius Cove in Sydney Harbour, a new style of Australian painting was emerging. With Tom Roberts and Arthur Streeton, Henry Fullwood founded the New South Wales Society of Artists in 1895. He also began to practise etching, a technique in which he was pioneer. However, the economic crisis within Australia incited him to return to London where, in 1901, he worked for the Graphic.

During the war Fullwood, too old to do active service, was employed at the London General Hospital of Wandsworth. In 1917 he was appointed as official painter and did two campaigns: the first from September to December of that year, the second from June to August 1918, with the 5th A.I.F. Division. He returned to Australia in 1920 and became a founder-member of the Painters-Engravers' Society. In his war works, Fullwood depicted the daily life of the soldiers and their places of manouevres. In contrast, his watercolour landscapes softened the harsh and difficult times.

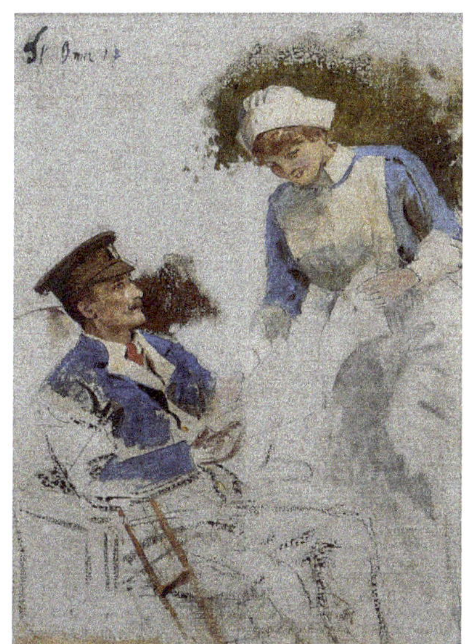

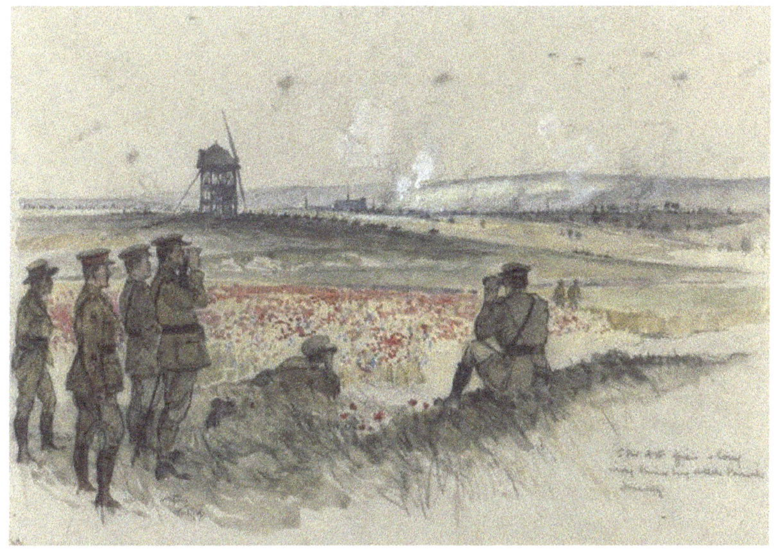

Henry Fullwod: *Wounded Officer in France*; *The AIF officers at Croisy being shelled* (AWM).

Fred Leist

Fred Leist[143] commenced as an illustrator for papers such as the *Bulletin* and the *Sydney Mail* He owed his first steps towards an artistic career to Julian Ashton. In 1908, he went to London and worked for the *Graphic.* At the beginning of the war, he was employed at the War Office. Later he was recruited as War Artist in the 5th A.I.F. Division where he met Henry Fullwood. Fred Leist was one of the most productive artists. His major works were commissioned and executed between 1918 and 1920, after the conflict. Returning to Australia in 1926, he pursued a career as a professor at East Sydney Technical College until 1938.

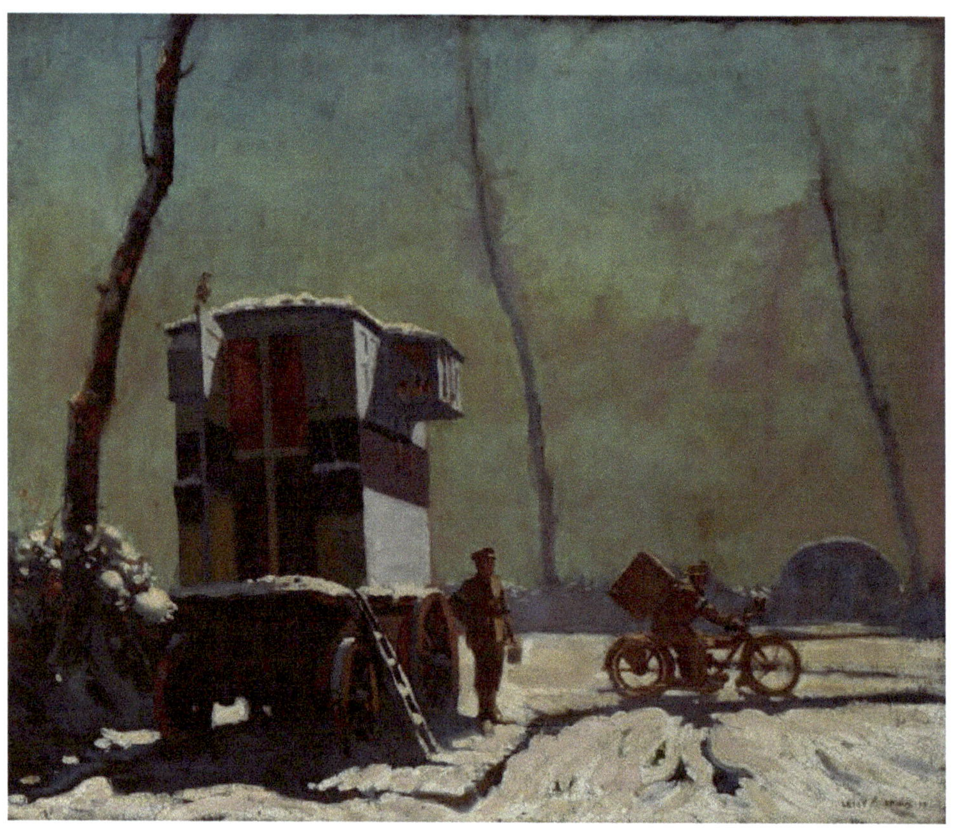

Fred Leist: *The Pidgeon Loft,* 1917. Art Gallery of NSW.

Isobel Rae

In June 1916, the battle of the Somme was raging. More and more British troops were drawn into the conflict and the Etaples Camp grew considerably. It was a point of regroupment and a training centre for troops before advancing to the Front, as well as an important hospital complex.

Without being recruited by the military authority, Isobel Rae recorded those times of war in numerous pastels which, more than the official paintings, give a good idea of daily life behind the scenes. Pastels offered her wide scope yet a simple and economic medium, points to be appreciated in a time of scarcity.

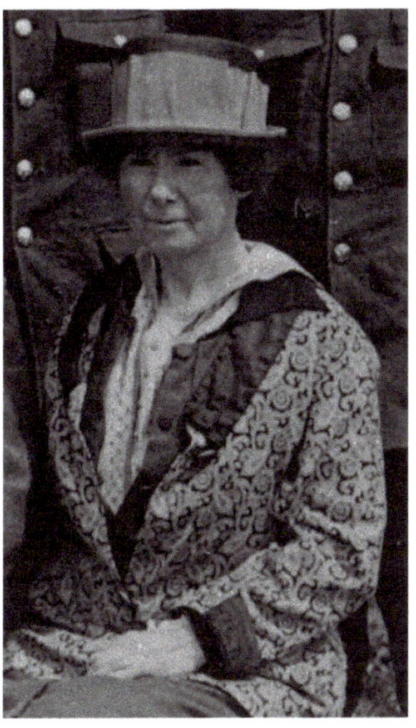

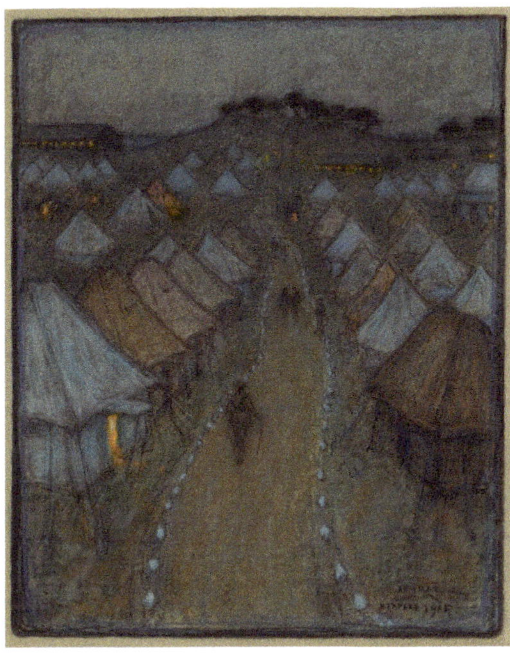

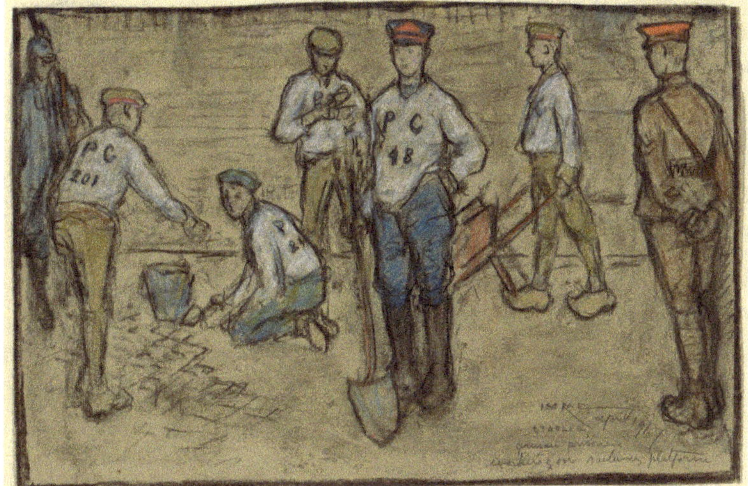

Isobel Rae, Etaples 1915.

Isobel Rae: *Etaples, 1915.*

Isobel Rae: *German Prisoners of War, 1917.*

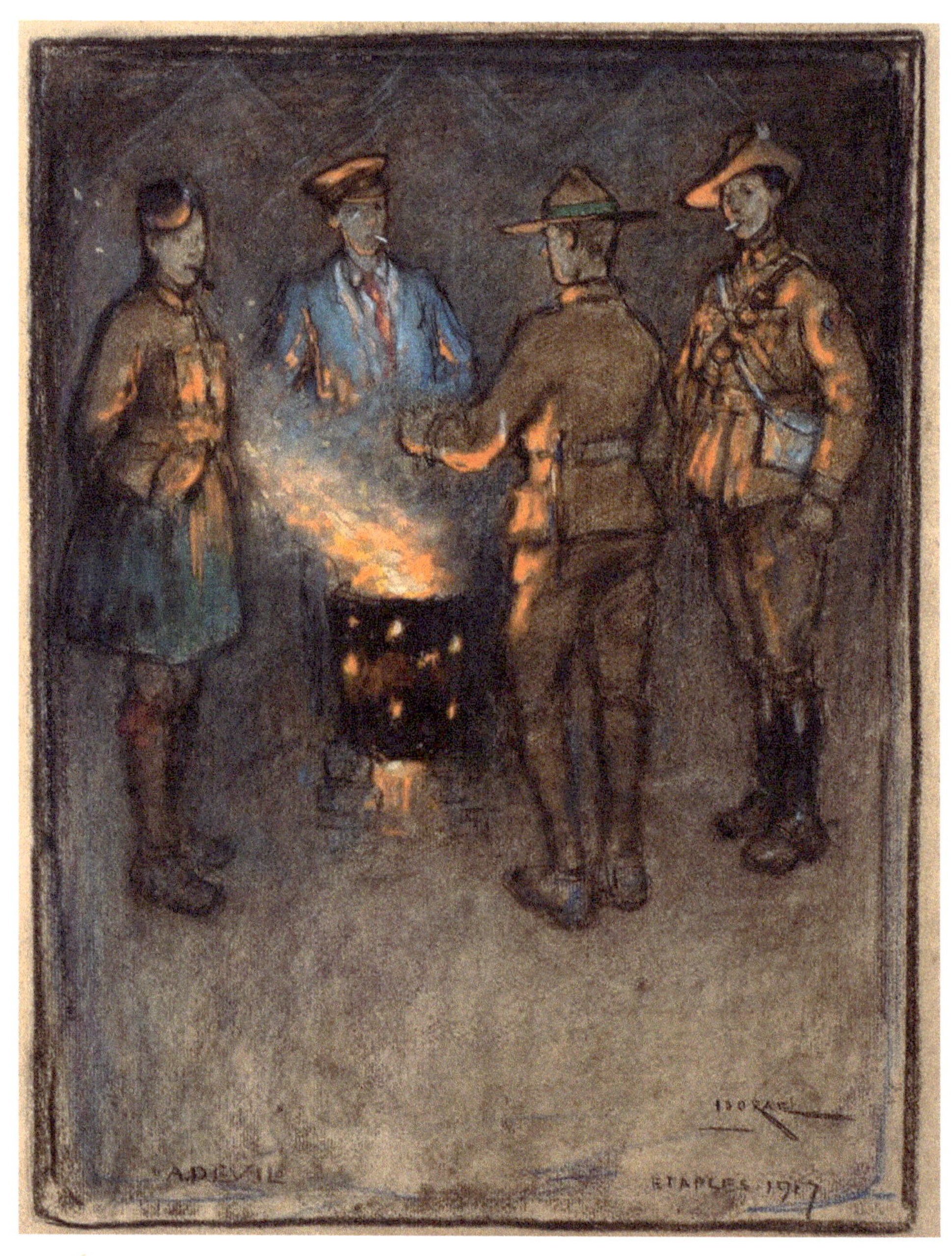

Isobel Rae: *A Devil.* Etaples 1917.

Arthur Streeton

With Tom Roberts and Frederick McCubbin, Arthur Streeton[144] was one of the prominent figures of the new Australian painting at the end of the 19th c. He studied at the National Gallery School, Melbourne, and was one of the famous Heidelberg pioneer painters. But artistic boldness is rarely accompanied by material comfort, especially in times of conservatism and economic crisis. Arthur Streeton therefore moved to Sydney and in the company of Tom Roberts, painted the harbour, Sirius Cove and Manly. It was a time when life was cheap and rough, a time of new approaches to painting, discoveries and enthusiasm. He visited Egypt in 1897 and travelled between Australia - where his fame was confirmed, and England - where recognition of his talent was slower. This fine landscapist, able to render a depth of atmosphere and "to awaken Australians to the natural beauty of their country" with his palette of blues and gold, produced paintings which were the epitome of the Australian landscape.

During the First World War, Streeton worked at first at the London Hospital of Wandsworth with Tom Roberts and Henry Fullwood. He spent two difficult years there and the daily horrors of the injured, prepared him to confront other realities even more tragic. He was recruited war artist from 14 May to 13 August 1918 to the 2nd A.I.F. Division. His contract stipulated that he furnish at least twenty-five drawings and watercolours and after this period that he execute a large work of an operation in which the A.I.F. were engaged. Amiens, the Key of the West, a monumental work was the outcome and it hangs proudly in the Australian War Memorial, Canberra. He served a second time, from 17 October to 20 November 1918 and, largely exceeded the clause of his contract, producing more than one hundred watercolours.

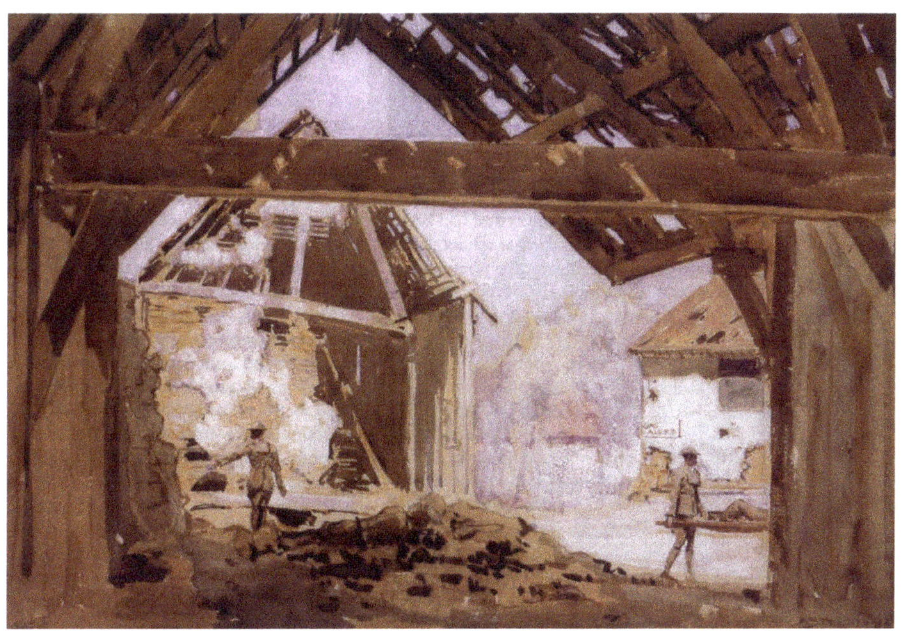

Arthur Streeton: *Gas Alert*. 1918. Australian War Memorial.

"Arriving in Boulogne, I reported, and was sent to St Martin for gas training and learnt how to discard the steel helmet and adjust my gas mask within three seconds, then to walk about a long room filled with the sickly sweet odour of chlorine; air oneself outside, and suddenly scatter to avoid a Gotha circling overhead."[145]

Streeton's drawing returns to the panoramic format of his Sydney scenes. It gives a good idea of troop movements within the port. In the background: the fish market and the cathedral dominate the old city.

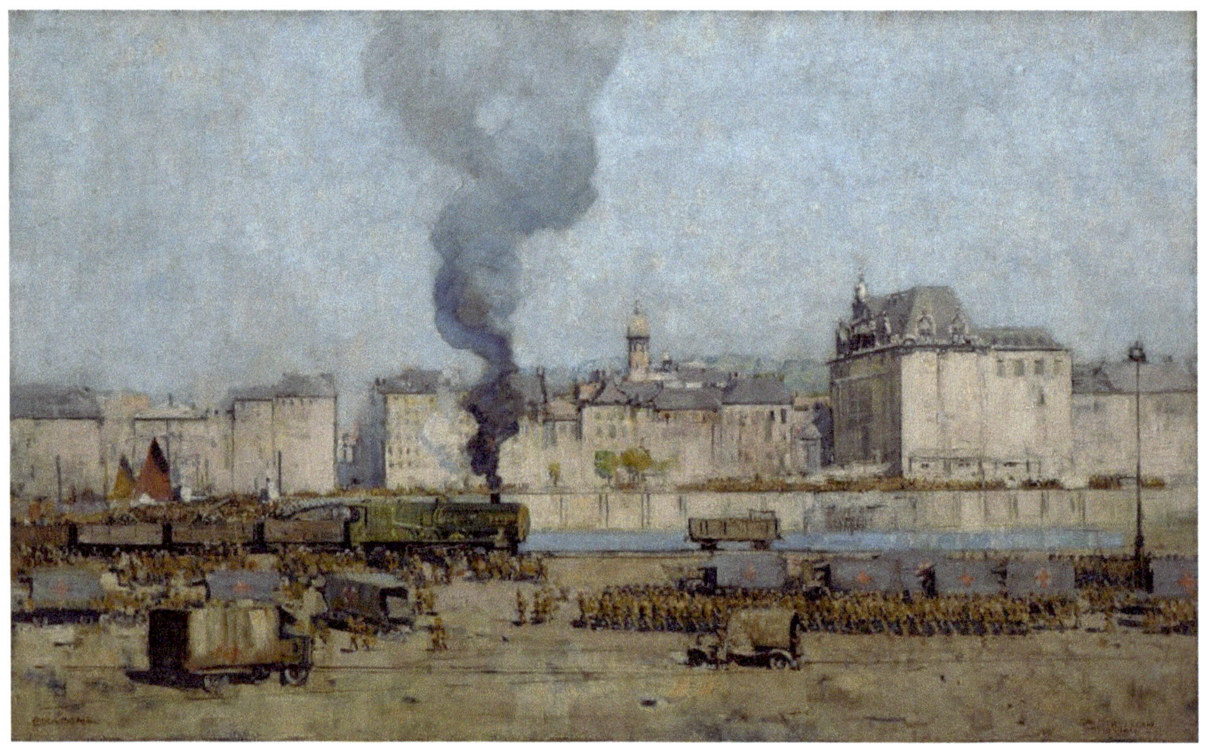

Arthur Streeton: *Boulogne.* 1918. Art Gallery of New South Wales.

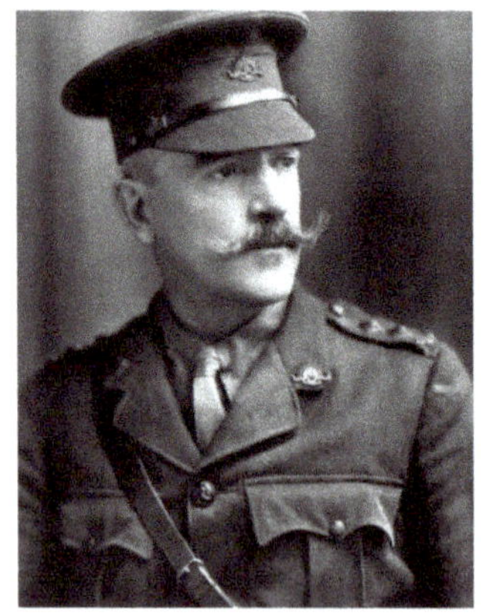

Endnotes

1] Fernand Holuigue (1905-1987).

2] Augustus Koopman (1869-1914) , American painter; stayed at Etaples and Equihen (nr Boulogn e-sur-Mer).

3] Harry Van der Weyden (1868-19 52), American painter at Moncreuil-sur-Mer.

4) Henry Ossawa Tanner (1859 -1937), Black American painter; stayed at Trépied (near Etaples).

5] Period before France became a republic

6] Eugene von Guerard (1812-1901) & Nicolas Chevalier (1828-1902). Painters/explorers drawn to Australia by the discovery of gold ; they painted large landscapes in the course of expeditions into the interior of the continent.

7] Frederic Edwin C hurch {1826-1900) & Albert Bierstadt (1830-1902). American painters ; they painted the early landscapes of North America - Niagara, Rocky Mountains in grand, photographic style.

8] Between 1882 and 1891.

9] Louis Buvelor (1814-1888). The father of landscape painting and the first to reproduce the real character of the Australian landscape.

10] Girolamo Nerli (1860-1926). Italian impressionist who lived in Australia and New Zealand

11] John Longstaff was the first to benefit by this system in 1887.

12] Alison Rae, *The Australian,* 14 March 1891.

13] Rix Archives.

14] *The Age,* 1 July 1899.

15] Jean-Claude Lesage, *Peintres des Cotes du Pas-de-Calais,* AMME Editions, Etaples 1987.

16] Writing desk.

17] Alison Rae, "An Old House in Etaples", *The Australian,* 9 May 1891.

18] Birge Harrison (1854-1 929). American painter, husband of Australian, Eleanor Ritchie.

19] Elsie Rix, ''An Artists' Colony in Picardy", *The Home,* 1 March 1922.

20] Pierre-Emmanuel Damoye (1847-1916), French landscapist. Karl Daubigny (1846-1886), French marine painter. Eugène Boudin (1824-1898), French landscapist.

21] Rix Archives.

22] Birge Harrison, "In Search of Paradise with Camera and Palme", *Outing,* January 1893.

23] Rix Archives.

24] Henri Duhem (1860-1941), French landscapist. Louis Paul Dessar (1867-1952), American painter of the Tonal School.

25] Eugene Chigoc (1860-1923), French painter and leading figure of the Etaples School. Louis Le Sidaner (1862-1939), French landscape and still-life painter.

26] Frits Thaulow (1847-1906), Norwegian painter, Gauguin's brother in law.

27] "Hote l des Voyageurs", opposite Eraples rail station, owned by Mr Maure.

28] Le journal de Montreuil, 11 & 18 August 1892, & Paris-Plage, 7 August 1892.

29J Dates of exhibitions of which a trace has been kept: 1896, 1898, 1904 (cat.), 1909, 1910 (car.), 1911 (cat.), 1912, 1913 (cat.), 1914 (car.).

30] Paris-Plage, 18 July 1909.

31] In 1909 & 1910, A. D. Turner (American) was president of exhibitions; in 1911, H. Boddington (English); in 1912 , G. Senseney (American) and in 1913 & 19 14 , H. O. Tanner (American).

32] In 1914, eighty nine painters exhibited 223 works.

33] Text reported by W Moore, Australian arc critic, NGA Archives, Canberra.
34] Jean-Paul Laurens (1828- 1921).
35] Theophile Alexandre Steinlen (1859-1923). Painter and lithographer; he illustrated works by J. Rictus, J.Renard, A. France, J . Richepin
36] Paris-Plage, 19 August 1911.
37] "A small colony of artists still remains at Etaples: Mr and Mrs Austen Brown, Miss Rae, Miss How, Mr Baker Clack." (*Colour,* February 1916).
38] *The Home*, September 1926.
39) Jules Wengel (1865-1934), German painter in Montreuil.
40] Exhibited Salon 1908.
41] The Royal Academy, London: a conservative institution which stayed outside the artistic trends. It had the advantage of offering its members both social position and the assurance of sales.
42] Max Bohm (1868-1923) , also stayed in Etaples.
43] Gustave Jeffroy, in *Catalogue d'exposition R. Bunny.* Galerie G. Petit, Paris 1917.
44] Alphonse Legros (1837-1911), French engraver.
45] *L'Ain a Champagnole,* Salon des Artistes Français, 1899.
46] Rupert Bunny, sketchbooks. Ref. 1948.28, 1948.31, 1948.32. University of Melbourne Art Gallery, Melbourne.
47] Letter from Etaples, 31 July 1902. I thank Mary Eagle for access to this letter.
48] List of villas, Le Moniteur de Paris-Plage, N°15, August-September 1905.
49] Colette Reddin, *Rupert Bunny Himself - His Final Years in Melbourne,* Melbourne 1987.
50] C. Langdale, Monotypes by Maurice Prendergast, Terra Museum, Chicago, 1984.
51] Helen, the Koopmans' daughter. She was then 4 years old.
52] Fries Thaulow, Les Moulins de Montreuil. In. C. Lesage, op. cit.
53] *Le Figaro*, 14 April 1910.
54] Atheneum, N° 8, 1928.
55] James (1854), Catherine (1856), Jean (1857), Alison (1858), Isobel (1860).
56] Janet Rae's death certificate, 7August 1916, (Council Archives, Etaples).
57] *Argus* (Melbourne), 20 December 1884; *The Age* (Melbourne), 26 April 1887.
58] On the theme of "the lost child", see L. Astbury, *City Bushmen.* Oxford University Press, Melbourne 1985.
59] Gustave Courcois (1852- 1923); Pascal Adolphe Jean Dagnan-Bouveret (1852-1929).
60] Jules Bastien-Lepage (1848-1884).
61] Alison Rae. "Australian Artists in Paris," *The Australasian,* 14 March 1891.
62] Letter, 18 July 1890. Bohm Papers, AAA, Washington DC.
63] Quoted by Gsell, *La Revue Bleue*, 3 September 1892.
64] Situated in the garages of the Hotel du Lion d'Argent, Place d'Etaples
65] Letter in French to Achille Caron, 8 April 1937. Societe Academique du Touquet.
66] Exhibited in Dunedin, (NZ), at the South Seas and New Zealand Exhibition, 1890.
67] Eugene Chigot, *La Procession de la barque miraculeuse de St-Josse* (*The Procession of the Miraculous Boat of St-josse),* Musee d'Arras. Jules Breton, Les communiantes (The Girls' Communion), Perth, GB.
68] Grand Larousse XXth c., Paris 1933.
69] Melbourne 1858 - after 1934
70] December 1904, National Library of Australia, Canberra.

71] Hilda Rix: "An Artist's Life in Paris", *The Home*, March 1922.
72] Near Bd Montparnasse , an area crowded with artists' studios.
73] Richard Miller (1875-1943).
74] Jules Adler, French painter (1865-1952).
75] Etaples colony painters travelled to the Middle East: Tanner to Morocco, Egypt and the Holy Land; Ethel Carrick-Fox to Morocco, and Ada Collier to Tunisia.
76] Letter, 4 February 1912 from Gibraltar. Harry Van der Weyden wrote her from Montreuil, the letters crossing: "Dear Angel! What has become of you? We are awaiting your news. Have you been devoured by cannibals - pouah!"
77] Gil Blas, 21 November 1912. It was Louis Vauxcelles who termed "fauves", the works exhibited in the Salon d'Automne in 1905
78] Major Nicholas of the 24th Batallion was killed at Fiers (between Albert and Bapaume) leading his men onto the battlefield. He was 29.
79] 1866-1947.
80] James Ashton (1859-1935); one of the founders of South Australian artistic life.
81] The *Bulletin*, Sydney, 19 November 1908.
82] She visited Tremalo, Concarneau, Ponc-Aven, Quimper and Royan in 1909 and 1910.
83] Lefawc Farm, Montreuil Church Portal, Saint-Josse Interior .
84] John Dowie, one of Marie Tuck's students. The Advertiser, Adelaide, 17 February 1971.
85] Jean-François Millet (1814-1875); Jules Breton (1827-1906); Jules Bastien-Lepage (1848-1884); Leon Lhermitte (1844-1925).
86] Eanger Irving Couse (1866-1936).
87] *L'Album Couse*, AMME Editions, p. 23.
88] Romanesque edifice destroyed during the Second World War.
89] Fitzroy, Melbourne, 1869 - Sydney, 1936
90] Julian Ashton (1851-1942).
91] "A Young Australian Artist - Back from Paris - A Chat with Miss Muskett," *Daily Telegraph*, 26 June 1897.
92] London 1868 - Melbourne 1960.
93] Charles Lasar (1856-1936).
94] Constance Jenkins (1883-1961).
95] Bernard Hall (1859-1935).
96] 1892-1942.
97] *Sydney Morning Herald*, 16 May 1919.
98] Ipswich, Qld, 1868 - Brisbane, 1961.
99] *A Century of Australian Women Artists 1840-1940*. Deutscher Fine Art Gallery, Malvern, Vic., 1993.
100] 1869-1946.
101] 10 June 1909. In Letters from Frances Hodgkins. Auckland University Press, 1993.
102] Ben Nicholson (1894-1982); Barbara Hepworth (1903-1975).
103] 1865-195
104] The Montreuil pig market, renowned in the area, was held in the Place Sr Jacques.
105] 1882-1957.
106] Fitzroy, Vic., 12 March 1865 - Melbourne, 8 October 1915.
107] Letter to Tom Roberts, Etaples, 30 July 1887.

108] Alexander Harrison (1853-1930).
109] American painter. In Etaples in 1887 where he painted Le Marchi d'Etaples. Musèe Quentovic, Etaples.
110] Louis Le Sidaner. French painter, Musèe Quentovic, Etaples.
111] London, 24 October 1868 - Virginia Water, Surrey, 9 February 1909.
112] Letter of 6 June 1890, quoted in *Table Talk*, 1 August 1890.
113] Pierre Puvis de Chavannes (1824-1898).
114] Louis Anquetin (1861- 1932).
115] At the Moulin Rouge, At the Ambassador; Private Room.
116] Painting now in the Musee d'Art Moderne de Paris.
117] Walter Sickert (1860-1942); Aubrey Beardsley (1872-1898); Jacques-Emile Blanche (1861-1942).
118] Grace Joel, Dunedin, NZ, 26 May 1865 - London, 6 March 1924.
119] Elizabeth Nourse (1859-1938), American; Beatrice How (1867-1932), English; Virginie Demont (1859-1935), French.
120] Confirmed by Liz Jerram, the artist's great niece (letter, 18 March 1999).
121] Murray Downs Station NSW, 19 September 1871 - Macedon NSW, 7 July 1921.
122] *Sun*, Melbourne, 11 December 1896.
123] Melbourne, 4 December 1869 - Prahan Vic., 18 February 1951.
124] 1854-1895.
125] She exhibited Cherry Time, at the 1888 Salon.
126] Argus, 30 April 1888.
127] Darlinghurst NSW, 16 June 1858 - Randwick, NSW, 30 April 1930.
128] Alphonse Legros (1837-1911).
129] Jean-Charles Cazin (1841-1901). French painter, friend and fellow artist of Legros.
130] J. P. Russell, *Nude Woman*, sanguine on blueish paper.
131) Emile Bernard (1868-1941).
132] Armand Guillaumin (1841-1927).
133] 5 October & 26 December 1887.
134] Marianna Mattiocco (1865-1908), model of sculptor Harry Bares. She became Russell 's companion and then his wife in 1888.
135] Claude Monet was at Belle-lle (Brittany) from September to November 1886 where he painted more than a dozen works.
136] Alison Rae, "Australian Artists in Paris", *The Australasian*, 14 March 1891.
137] Finchley GB, 28 April 1862 - London, 21 December 1906.
138] Australian and New Zealand Army Corps.
139] Enmore NSW, 1883 - Manly NSW, 1937.
140] Will Ashton (1881-1963), leading Sydney art figure.
141] Alfredtown Vic., 3 September 1880 - London, 21 January 1938.
142] Birmingham, 15 March 1863 - Sydney, 1 October 1930.
143] Fred Leist, Sydney, 1878-1945
144] Mt Duneed Vic., 8 May 1867 - Olinda Vic., 2 September 1943.
145] A. Streeton, "Great War through an Artist's Eyes", *Melbourne Herald*, 25 April 1936.

INDEX

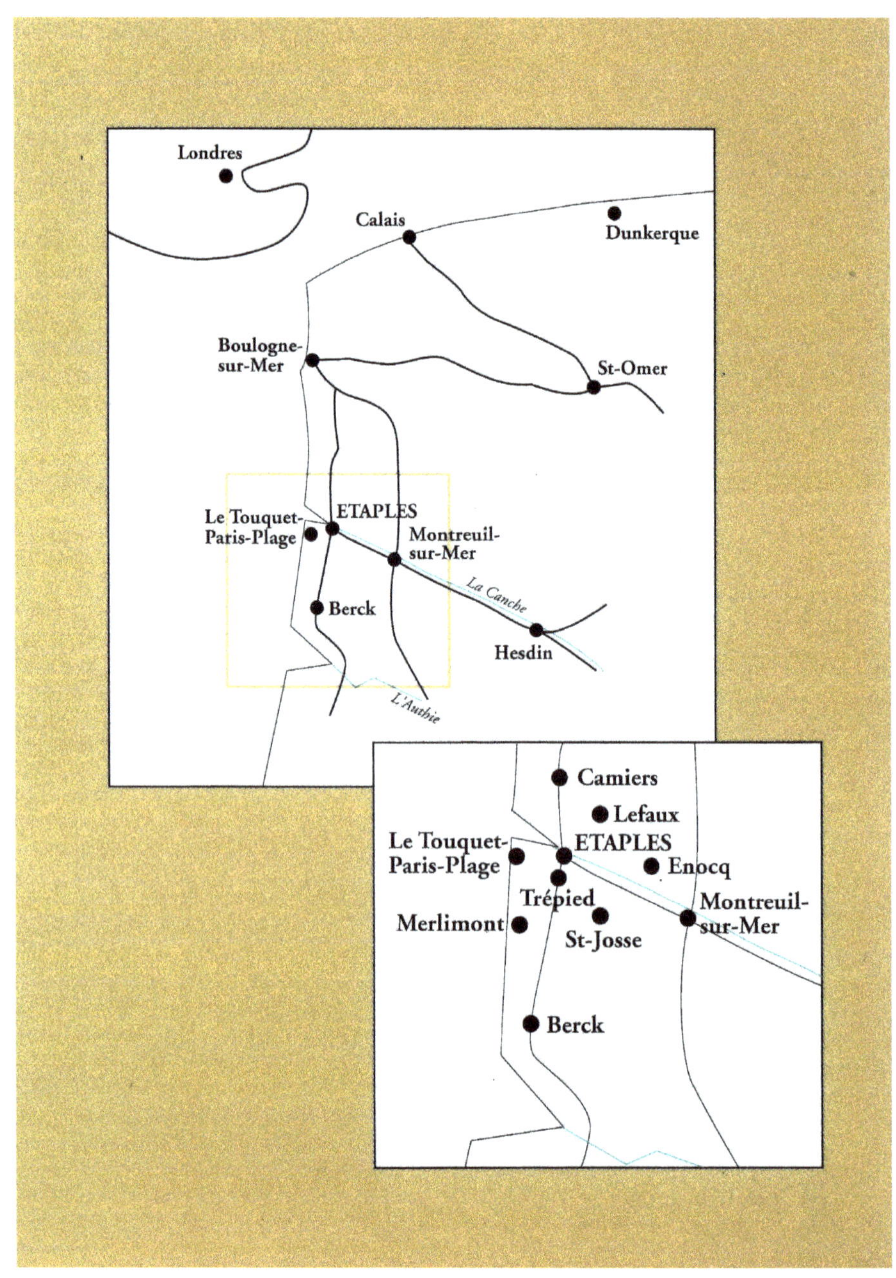
Londres
Calais
Dunkerque
Boulogne-sur-Mer
St-Omer
Le Touquet-Paris-Plage
ETAPLES
Montreuil-sur-Mer
La Canche
Berck
Hesdin
L'Authie
Camiers
Lefaux
Le Touquet-Paris-Plage
ETAPLES
Enocq
Trépied
Montreuil-sur-Mer
Merlimont
St-Josse
Berck